# Praise for the Min

'Astonished' does not begin to describe ho
Tonya, an incredibly confident, positive, and empowering woman, had such a tumultuous adolescence. This is precisely why Mindset Switch is one of the most important books I've read. She not only persevered to become a successful entrepreneur amidst adversity, but she was also able to shift her perspective to create a beautiful, forward-thinking life. Whether you're living the life of your dreams, or are unsure where to begin, *Mindset Switch* is a must read for all.

—Gina Ferwerda
Michigan Resort Owner & Author

Tonya has an amazing way of putting people instantly at ease, allowing them to be vulnerable and open to deep mindset work without it hurting at all. Her authentic "girlfriend" coaching style comes straight through the pages of this book, as if she's right there in the room with you. Drawing from her own incredible life experiences as well as those of the many women she's worked with, Tonya will capture your heart as she guides you on a remarkable do-it-yourself journey to transforming your mindset. If you're looking for a book that will elevate you to the next level and help you find aligned success and passion in everything you do, this book is a must-read!

—Nicole Holland, Modern Marketing Specialist and Host of the Business
Building Rockstars Show

Tonya Rineer is my go-to girl when it comes to mindset. She is the perfect combination of all things science with a hint of woo-woo. We don't realize how detrimental our limiting beliefs are to designing a life we love. Make sure to read this book if you are looking to live the life you've always dreamed of. The new you is waiting for you to discover your full potential.

—Stacy Tuschl, Entrepreneur, #1 International Bestselling Author,
Host of the top rated podcast on iTunes - She's Building Her Empire

# The Mindset Switch

The Mindset Switch is published by Kat Biggie Press.
http://katbiggiepress.com

Cover design by Michelle Fairbanks, Fresh Design
Editing by Liz Thompson, House Style Editing
Interior design by Write|Publish|Sell


ISBN-13: 978-0-9987779-9-3
Library of Congress Control Number: 2017954618
First Edition: March 2018


10 9 8 7 6 5 4 3 2 1

# Dedication

*To my husband, Tom, for supporting me even when you didn't understand me.*
*To my sons, Kyle, Matthew, and Tommy, for your encouragement and unwavering confidence in me.*
*To my sister, Danelle, for being my rock and mirror and always having my back.*
*I'll never be able to put into words how much I love and appreciate you. XO*


*In loving memory of my mom, Sally Ann. I miss you everyday.*

# Contents

## Part 1

## Part 2

## Part 3

# Foreword

What do you believe? I believe that any human being can overcome seemingly insurmountable adversity and start living life to their fullest potential; we simply need a roadmap to show us how. Tonya Rineer's book, Mindset Switch, is your roadmap.

When I first met Tonya at the Best Year Ever Blueprint event, a few years ago, I intuitively felt that she was one of those change-makers that I would be hearing about for years to come. But more than that, I believed in what she stood for – empowering people to rise above their fears and limitations, to create a life that they're in love with.

In *The Mindset Switch*, you're going to discover what's standing between you and your next-level life. Tonya gives practical tips and the guidance needed to recognize what's holding you back, so that you can unlock your greatest potential. Whether you're looking to improve your finances, health, relationships, spirituality or business – you'll quickly find that her message is universally applicable.

I also believe in the power of words. And I agree with Tonya that in order to create lasting change, we must become aware of the way we talk—about the world around us, to the people in our lives, and to ourselves.

Our words create our reality. That's why I include the use of daily affirmations as one of the essential elements in my book, The Miracle Morning. Affirmations are a tool for shifting the way you perceive yourself, and the world around you, so that you can create more of what you want in every area of your life.

I love the way Tonya explains the various factors that contribute to our belief system as layers, with words being the easiest to recognize and transform and then going deeper into how those words affect our thoughts, feelings and actions.

Throughout the Mindset Switch, you're going to experience a series of breakthroughs and ah-ha moments as you learn how to transform your thoughts, feelings and ultimately your beliefs about yourself, your life and the possibilities that are available to you.

Tonya has taken her own powerful story of transformation, combined it with her years of research and professional experience as a mindset coach, and mixed in relatable stories, to create this practical guidebook for creating change. If I could say one thing about this book, it's this: It is results-oriented and fluff-free. What I mean is that it is a tool for change. It will help you discover what's been holding you back and give you the resources you need to break through to the next level of your epic life!

As soon as you get intentional about the improvements you want to make in your life, you'll start to experience the breakthroughs that lead to results. When you take control of your own mindset – your words, thoughts, feelings and beliefs – there are no limits on what you can achieve.

You have the desire in your heart, and now you have the roadmap in this book. You are literally holding everything you need to make change happen in your life. Now it's up to you to take action. Most importantly, I believe in you.

—Hal Elrod

Author of *The Miracle Morning*, Executive Producer of *The Miracle Morning MOVIE*, and host of the *Achieve Your Goals* Podcast.

# Introduction

Do you believe that everything happens for a reason? I do. I believe that what you need will always find its way to you. You picked up this book for a reason. Something is missing in your life. Something that your soul is longing for. Something bigger and wildly abundant that is waiting for you right around the corner. The only thing standing between you and whatever that "something" is, is you. Or, more specifically, your mindset.

This book is going to help you identify and transform the limiting beliefs that are blocking you from all the abundant possibilities that await you so that you can get serious about what you want and take action toward making it happen. Don't worry; I'm going to give you the tools you need to do it all with ease.

I'm excited and honored to travel along on this journey with you. My greatest wish is that the information in this book is as transformational for you as it has been for me, and the many people I've had the privilege of sharing it with.

You might be wondering what kind of an impact this will really make on your life. All I can say is this: just try it! Give it a good, honest and consistent effort. Once you start to feel a shift in your energy, you'll get to witness your desires begin to manifest right before your eyes and start to see what can only be described as miracles happening everywhere.

I wasn't always a believer. In fact, I was a big-time skeptic of mindset work at first. It all sounded a little too "woo" to me. So if you're in the same camp, wondering if this is going to work for you, this book is a perfect introduction, as there is a healthy balance of practicality throughout. I promise not to go too woo on you!

If, however, you've been on the mindset bandwagon for a while, this book is going to help you take your practice to the next level and beyond. That's because I take everything you already know about positive mindset and the Laws of Attraction and Vibration and put it into a repeatable system you can implement again and again to get the results you want.

Whether you're a mindset newbie or a seasoned vet, you'll find a tremendous amount of value in this book, and I look forward to helping you ditch your limits and take control of the life you've been dreaming about and totally deserve.


Cheers to a mind-blowing journey,

The power to shift
our reality lies
in the ability
to shift
our focus.

# Chapter 1
## The Secret Behind the Switch

*Lack of self-worth killed my mom.*

Self-worth is the feeling that you are a valuable person who deserves to be treated with respect. Can you really die if you don't have that?

Her doctors may have said that it was pneumonia that did it. Or heroin. But I know her death started long before that.

Strangely enough, her ending marked my true beginning. It set me on the journey that caused me to change my life dramatically. It led me to the work I do now, helping others cultivate a strong sense of value within themselves, kick their limiting beliefs to the curb, and create the life-altering mindset shifts that redefine what's possible and make the wildest of dreams come true.

The concept of mindset management wasn't one I grew up with. I come from a family that believed themselves to be realists and rejected anything that wasn't considered mainstream. And at that time, mindset wasn't a topic that people openly discussed, at least not in my world.

My grandparents were both entrepreneurs who grew up during the Depression and were always afraid of not having enough. My grandpa lived on potatoes for most of his childhood. Literally, nothing but potatoes! That's the kind of stuff that gets embedded into your brain and is hard to forget. As they grew up, no matter how much they had, there was always that fear that— at any moment— the bottom was going to fall out. That they could be left, once again, with nothing. In their minds, scarcity was everywhere.

They didn't want their children to experience that same struggle and pain. So they made sure they did their best to protect my mom and her five siblings from scarcity by ensuring they always had everything they ever needed and wanted.

Easy street became a way of life for my mom. All she had to do was bat her eyelashes at my grandpa, and she got whatever she wanted. But that came at a price. She learned that the way to get ahead was to attach yourself to someone who had the means to give you what you wanted. She didn't grow up learning how to empower herself. Instead, she grew up depending on others to feel safe and cared for.

She was beautiful. Like drop-dead gorgeous. She was one of those people that could walk into a room and, instantly, everyone was drawn to her positive, magnetic energy. No matter what awkward grouping of people was there, she could always make everyone feel comfortable and have everyone laughing together in minutes. So many people adored her, and everyone loved to be around her.

But that's not how she saw herself.

She thought she was fat, even though she was probably 115 pounds soaking wet. She battled constant eating disorders and addictions to diet supplements. She was always trying to fix the person she saw in the mirror, attempting to achieve "perfection" and searching for love and admiration in return.

My parents divorced when I was eleven. My dad all but disappeared, and my mom had a hard time paying the bills alone. It was during this transition that I started to notice the effect of her disempowering beliefs.

There she was: a single mother, with two daughters, a mortgage, a stack of bills she couldn't pay, and little love for herself. What she needed most was to feel independent and strong, but all she felt was lost, confused, and broken. In that critical "turn lemons into lemonade" time of her life, all she could bring herself to see was the rotten-ass lemons in front of her.

And because the money lesson she had learned over and over was to attach herself to someone who had money . . . that's where she focused her energy. She started to attract wealthy men who were all about their status and ego: celebrities, athletes, and successful businessmen.

On the outside, these men had it all— good looks, money, and fame. But they were also verbally abusive, manipulative, and big-time players. It was hard to watch. Even as a young girl, I knew she didn't believe she was enough. She didn't believe she was capable of landing a man who could take care of her financially and would treat her right. She believed she had to choose, one or the other. She chose security.

At the age of 13, I watched her wealthy boyfriend mentally, emotionally, and verbally abuse her. He was always trying to make her his perfect little Barbie doll to show off to his friends— forcing her to train at the gym, paying for breast implants, insisting she keep up her appearance at all costs—but in his eyes, she was never perfect enough. She always fell short. He acted as though her lack of perfection embarrassed him. He manipulated her, said demeaning and belittling things about her to his friends—pinching her hips and calling her "meaty," poking fun at her cooking, belittling her "pathetic little waitressing job," calling her stupid, fat, slow, washed-up—right in front of her. Thinking about it still makes me sick.

When you're already in a dark place, it doesn't take a whole lot of that kind of abuse before you start to feel hopeless and believe other people when they tell you that you will never be enough. You start to believe that you really are worthless. I see it happen all the time. I watched it happen to my mom. He chipped away repeatedly at her soul. It wasn't that she felt worthless—a feeling that is temporary, and in time it goes away. No, she believed she was worthless. This became her state of being. Her identity.

She found her own way to cope, though, thanks to friends who were high-functioning heroin addicts, and began to self-medicate.

That's when everything started to spin out of control. By the time I was fifteen, my mom was a full-on addict living in a shady hotel room, and I was homeless. Left to run the streets, alone. I spent that summer doing things no teenage girl should witness, let alone experience—drinking in biker bars, going to all-night raves, hanging around with gangs, experimenting with drugs—if it was a bad idea, I was probably doing it. I was on a downward spiral at full speed!

*And then, I got pregnant.*

You'd think I would have been terrified to tell my mom. I wasn't actually; maybe because I hoped it would give her a distraction. Something to focus on and look forward to. I sat her down, looked her in the eyes and said: "Mom, I'm pregnant." She looked away and just stared off into space, without blinking, for what had to be the longest minute of my life. When she finally looked back at me, she said, "Now I have something to live for, don't I?"

A mix of emotions washed over me at that moment. I felt shocked, angry, hurt and helpless all at the same time. I remember thinking, *"You've got to be kidding me! Aren't I enough to live for? Don't I mean anything?"* But what cut me even deeper was the realization that she didn't believe she was enough.

She didn't believe she had enough to offer the world. She didn't believe that she deserved the life she dreamed of. And she didn't believe she had the strength to fight the drug addiction that was threatening to kill her.

Five days after telling her I was pregnant, even after declaring that she now had a reason to live, my mom gave into the temptation to get high one more time. That "one more time," turned out to be her last.

Two months before my sixteenth birthday, and six months before I would become a mother myself, my mom passed away.

I probably should have become a statistic. That's what everyone expected me to do—get on welfare, drop out of school, and give up on myself. I could see it in their eyes when they looked at me. My aunts, uncles, grandparents, everyone expected me to be a failure. But I saw, first hand, what happens when limiting beliefs take hold, and you allow yourself to believe that the negative perceptions of the people around you. I decided that I would never lose faith in myself the way my mom did. I wanted more for my life. And despite what everyone else thought, I was going to get it.

Having my son helped me discover what I really wanted, which was to be the best mom I could be. It gave me the motivation to prove everybody around me wrong. I refused to be a high-school dropout or a teen mom welfare case, even though that's what most people I knew were betting on.

I remember those moments well. Overhearing whispers from the next room, the dirty looks that they tried to conceal. It was as though I had shamed them. I remember thinking, *"Screw you people! Where were you when I was living on the streets? You weren't around to help me, and now you're judging me!? Ha! Let me show you what I can do without you!"*

Don't get me wrong; it's not like I was completely alone. I did have the emotional support of a few close friends and family members, and I am filled with gratitude for those wonderful people. Financially, though, I was on my own. I rented an apartment, raised a baby, put myself through school, and I didn't need a handout to do it. Accomplishing that by myself felt empowering and validating; helping to shut out any fear or doubt about what I was capable of. I was so determined to succeed that I didn't give myself another option. I decided it was possible and that I was capable. And so it was.

And I'm freaking proud of who I became as a result of those decisions. But here's the kicker: my own mindset switch didn't noticeably happen until years later.

Yes, I had some stubborn motivation that got me through what could have been some pretty tough years.

But for nearly another decade I was caught in the same mindset trap as my family had been in for generations. My programming, everything I had been brainwashed to believe, told me I had to go to school, put in my time, and that I didn't get to enjoy wealth, freedom, and uninterrupted happiness until I retired.

I had a nagging feeling inside that there was more. I wanted more. I was conflicted with feeling selfish for wanting more while also not caring that I did. I had hope that things could be easier than they were, and that I was capable of something bigger. But I didn't understand how to make it happen, so I just kept telling myself that it wasn't in the cards for me. Abundance, freedom, wealth, and living a life of luxury was for the lucky and the privileged. It was for the people who were pre-qualified for success. The people who were let in on the "secrets" that I was not privy to.

So I did what I thought I was supposed to do. I went to school and got a degree (and then another one). I landed a cushy job with a decent salary and began my climb up the corporate ladder. I was living the "American Dream" . . . until I got laid off. Even though I enjoyed that job, the abrupt loss of income made me realize that the last thing I wanted was to continue to have my fate in someone else's hands. So I thought, *"I could start a business, right?"*

I had no clue, but I knew that If I didn't take the leap at that moment, I never would. So I jumped. I didn't know what the heck I was doing, but I just kept taking the next best step, making mistakes and learning lessons. Still, I was working my ass off and not making the money I wanted.

And I thought, *"This isn't what I want! Why am I stuck? How can I fix this?*

I don't like feeling stuck. I'm wired to need answers. So I started reading and researching (okay, obsessing) about what made successful people tick. What made them different? What secret did they know that I didn't? I was determined to figure it out.

That's when I discovered mindset work. It hooked me. I spent more than a year dedicating all of my spare time to learning everything I could find that was related to personal growth, spiritual development, positive psychology, conscious awakening and anything else that might be considered "woo-woo."

And because I'm an action taker, I started experimenting with what I was learning—meditation, affirmations, gratitude journaling, Emotional Freedom and Neuro-Linguistic Programming techniques—you name it, if it was suggested, I tried it. Sometimes the things I tried helped to propel me further toward my goals, and other times, not so much. I remember thinking, "Is this a joke or is this legit?" I doubted the Law of Attraction and all the woo-woo stuff more than a few times.

The problem was that it was all so philosophical. It was like all these people were saying, *"This beautiful world exists where there's everything you could ever want. Now go home and think about it on your meditation pillow and hopefully your intuition will lead you there."*

That didn't cut it for me. I wanted a damn map! So I re-read everything and looked for the consistencies and patterns in the advice being given until I found themes—practice gratitude and positive thinking, visualize, say affirmations, meditate, etc. But furthermore, I wanted to know why these practices worked for some and not others. What I found was that there is a proper order in which to incorporate these practices into your life. Doing them out of order lessens their effect. But in the proper order, the positive effects are compounded. That's when I realized that I had something concrete to work with and implement. I broke it all down to create a repeatable practice to make these big shifts happen OFF my meditation pillow. (Truthfully, I don't even own a freakin' meditation pillow.)

I did this for myself first and . . . OMG, it worked! Every. Single. Time!

I started sharing my practice with other people, and it worked for them too! They would go from feeling broken, hopeless, and less than enough; to feeling confident, empowered, and ready to take on the world. That's when I realized how powerful this work was, and decided that I could continue sharing this with people forever. Helping others transform their mindset (and empowering them to believe in what is possible for them) is definitely *My Thing*. My Purpose. I believe this is the reason behind everything that has happened in my life. I needed to experience the **mindset switch** for myself in order to teach it to others. And when I did, everything came into perfect alignment.

Since then, I've learned that while my mom's story is tragic and extreme, there are pieces of her story that resonate with so many people. She was nurturing, giving, and accommodating. She took care of everyone else first and rarely made herself a priority. If she had been able to look in the mirror and see what everyone else saw, things would have been different.

We all do this.

You do it too. You take care of everyone else and forget about yourself. You look in the mirror and focus on your flaws. You are painfully aware of your faults and your weaknesses. That's the mindset responsible for creating your limits, holding you back, and, ultimately, stealing your dreams out from under you. If you looked in the mirror and saw what everyone else sees, things would be different for you, too.

I know so many people who are strong and amazing. Yet they feel like they're not enough because they have never learned how to heal their mindset and truly value themselves.

You might feel this way. *You might not even know it.*

It shows up every time you wonder what people across the

room are whispering about. Every time you meet someone new and don't remember their name because you're already thinking about what you're going to say next. It's when you see someone attractive and think, "I wish I looked like that." It's when you drive past your dream home and think, "I want to live there," but at the same time feel it's out of reach for you. It's when you hesitate to wear a bathing suit because you're worried about being judged, or you're afraid to share your story because you're afraid that people won't relate to you, or worse, they'll reject you.

I know these feelings all too well.

I remember settling for mediocrity and "good enough." I was living that half-assed "American Dream" that had been passed on for generations. Because I didn't know any better.

That's just what we do. We follow the path that's been laid out for us. At least until we learn that there's another path. A better path. And that's when everything changes.

While I sat back and watched other people succeed—buy their dream home, go on extravagant vacations, and carry on without a care in the world—I kept thinking, *How are they doing that? What am I doing wrong? What's their secret?"*

Now, that I've figured it out, I can share it with you. The "secret" is that it's not a secret at all. It is a mindset.

And understanding that would have changed everything for my mom. She didn't feel important. She didn't feel worthy. She didn't feel like she had the power to create the life she wanted. And it cost her her life.

Everyone deserves to feel important. To believe that they are worthy.

I was too young to recognize what my mom was going through.

I wish I had because I knew how important and worthy she was. I wish I could have helped her see that.

I can't go back. But I know my experiences had a higher purpose. Because of the life I've lived, and what I've been through, I've gained some incredible knowledge on how to shift your mindset and dramatically change the course of your life.

I wasn't able to share this knowledge with my mom . . . but I can share it with you. And for that, I am honored and grateful.

You can create a life of your dreams. You can design it exactly the way you want it to be. And you can start right NOW. At this exact moment. All it takes is a little switch in the way your mindset works. Throughout this book (and by doing the exercises in the included workbook) I'm going to show you exactly how to flip that switch.

It might be tempting to skip around and read the parts that stick out to you most, but this book is set up to help you understand, break down, and reprogram your mindset in a way that is long-lasting and insanely effective. Think of it this way: It's not a mindset diet, it's a lifestyle change. So I encourage you to take the time to read through each part of the process and build the foundation that will transform your mindset. Trust me; there's a method to my madness.

In Chapter 2, I'll introduce you to the two mindsets, and you'll see how these mindsets have been influencing your thinking and causing your personal brand of self-sabotage.

In Chapter 3, we'll explore mindset as a concept and how it influences our thoughts, feelings, and behaviors. I'll also give you a crash course on reprogramming your brain and get the results you want.

In Chapter 4, you'll start to do the real work of identifying the things that trigger your negative mindset and limiting beliefs. You'll discover what's been holding you back and learn how to kick that crapola to the curb . . . like NOW.

In Chapters 5 through 9, we dig into the meat and potatoes of what it takes to flip the switch on your mindset. This is where I teach you the tricks and techniques to creating lasting change and getting repeatable results. These chapters are super action-oriented with a thorough explanation of the Mindset Switch layers that make up your programming (words, thoughts, feelings, and beliefs) and how to transform them via the Mindset Switch System. Plus, to double down on the action, I've included a workbook chock-full of activities, exercises and suggested mindset tools to make your mindset transformation easy, fun and a heck of a lot more powerful!

I am confident that this book is going to change your life. In fact, I'm pretty sure that you're going to be so geeked up about the results you start to see that you're going to want to teach this to everyone you know. (I know this because the same thing happened to me!) So, I've included a bonus section of Mastermind Questions in the back of this book to make that easy for you to do. Feel free to use these questions inside of your own group coaching program or mastermind, as a book club facilitation guide, or as journal prompts to deepen your learning experience.

And of course, if you'd like a place to deepen the discussion, get support or share ah-has and ideas, please join me inside my private Facebook group at: www.tonyarineer.com/facebook.

# Chapter 2
## Which Mindset Are You?

When it comes to mindset, there are only two: **limited mindset** and **growth mindset**.

As you read through this chapter, you might discover that you're currently operating in a limited mindset. Or maybe you waver between the limited and growth mindset. Either way, don't freak out. I'm going to guide you through making the switch into the mindset that will change everything.

I wavered between the two mindsets for years, depending on the situation. When it came to money, I was for sure in the limited mindset camp! Let me share a quick example before we dive in:

I used to believe that I was terrible at managing money. So I just avoided it. Why bother? I'm no good at it anyway. It's a waste of time. (Hello limited mindset!) Once I started a business, though, I quickly realized that my struggle with managing money was threatening to put me out of business. I knew that, since I couldn't afford to hire someone else to manage my books, I had to choose: Change my belief about my own capabilities or surrender my dream of being an entrepreneur. I chose me. I forced myself to read books and take classes until I figured it out. It didn't make me love it, but it did teach me the skills I needed to gain control of my money. I flipped the switch from a limited to a growth mindset, and it saved my business.

If you find that you, too, are stuck in a limited way of thinking in any area of your life—you don't know how you'll make as much money as you want, you don't know if you'll find the perfect partner, you doubt that you'll be able to make a significant difference in the world or any number of other beliefs that are limiting what is possible for you—this book is going to teach you how to change that. You're not just going to shift your mindset; you're going to go from wondering, "Can I do this?" to believing, "Hell, yes! I can absolutely do this!"

But first, we have to answer the question: **Which mindset are you?**

Let's start with the **limited mindset.** We sometimes refer to this way of thinking as a scarcity, lack, or negative mindset. Someone who subscribes to this way of viewing the world believes that abilities, skills, and possibilities are something you're born with or you're not. If you weren't gifted with the innate talent or ability that leads to success and abundance, then you're out of luck. It just isn't going to happen for you.

You might be living with a limited mindset if you:

- Worry (and sometimes stress) about what other people think
- Freak out about the possibility of failure and what it will say about you
- Try hard (really hard) to maintain a perfect I've-got-it-all-together appearance
- Worry about not having enough or getting your fair share
- Believe that success is a result of talent or luck.

You might even say things like:

*It's just not in the cards for me.*

*I've never had good luck.*

*It is what it is.*

*That'll never happen for me.*

*I'll just have to make the best of the hand I've been dealt.*

*It's a dog-eat-dog world out there.*

*I'd better take advantage of this while I can. Who knows how long this will last.*

Operating in a limited mindset means that you believe your fate is set and cannot be changed; that you don't have control over the results or outcome. You feel that you're stuck with what God or the Universe gave you.

A limited mindset is rooted in scarcity and restrictions. Fear that there will never be enough. Believing that you have to fight for what's yours. Hoard. Save. Conserve. Waste-not-want-not. Rush to get your share before it's all gone. People with a limited mindset spend lots (and lots) of time worrying about worst-case scenarios and fear of losing what they have been "lucky" enough to acquire.

That's not to say that those with a limited mindset are not successful, on the contrary, many are extremely successful. In fact, you might be, too. But underneath that success resides a deep, scary fear. The fear that you're going to lose it all. That someone is going to come along, who's better than you, and take your place. Take what you've worked so hard for. And leave you left wanting and wishing once again.

I bet you can think of more than a few people who were once at the top and then fell from glory. When you don't believe you deserve success or that it will run out . . . it eventually does. Plenty of celebrities, actors, athletes and regular joe schmoes have lost everything they once had because of this limited way of thinking.

Instead of taking chances, limited mindset folks would rather preserve their record of wins and play the blame game instead.

*I could have started my own business, but then I had kids and just didn't have the time.*
*I could have been an Olympic tennis player, but I sprained my wrist, and it ruined my game.*
*I could have gone to college but . . .*
*I could have . . . .*

Now, on the flip side of the coin, there is the **growth mindset**, also referred to as the abundance or positivity mindset. Those with a growth mindset, believe something entirely different.

These are people who believe anything is possible with a little effort! These folks have been accused (by limited thinkers) of looking at the world through rose-colored glasses and being overly positive, living in a fantasy world, or having unrealistic expectations. These people believe that the world is abundant and that there will always be enough to go around. They ask, and they receive. The way they view life can be summed up with the mantra: "Things always work out for me."

You might be living with a growth mindset if you:

- Believe that anything is possible for you
- Enjoy being challenged and learning new things
- Love the process of achieving as much as you love the achievement itself
- Have faith that there will always be enough of everything

you need

- Find strength in rising above challenges and persevering in the face of doubt

You might say things like:

*Everything happens for a reason.*
*There's always a silver lining.*
*You win some, you lose some, get up and try again.*
*It always works out in the end.*
*It's the journey that matters, not the destination.*
*It's not whether you win or lose, it's how you play the game.*
*This is happening for me, not to me. There is a lesson here.*

Operating in a growth mindset, you believe that every seemingly negative occurrence offers a deeper lesson and opportunity for personal growth and expansion. You believe in the power of positive focus and sustained effort. You know that your gifts, talents, and skills can be increased with practice and focus. You believe in yourself and what's possible.

You might still be afraid to take risks, but you manage to muster up the courage to get uncomfortable anyway. You fight through the fear. And when you fail (which inevitably happens) you consider it an opportunity for growth, search for the inherent lesson and use it to strengthen your resolve.

Think about Thomas Edison, Colonel Sanders, or Sara Blakely. What would have happened if they just gave up? If they believed their skills and abilities were fixed? Well, we wouldn't have electricity, KFC, or Spanx, that's for sure!

Upon considering the people I know, I can identify which

mindset they subscribe to. And sometimes it breaks my heart because I know those with a limited mindset have so much more to offer the world. But because they're stuck in fear, they continue to play small and stay comfortably within in their "zone of familiarity." My mom certainly had a limited mindset.

I meet people like my mom every day who, because of the lens through which they see the world, and themselves, aren't able to see the beauty, talent, and possibility that I see when I look at them.

What if my mom was able to flip her switch? And go from a limited mindset to a growth mindset?

What if she believed in herself enough to develop her skills and take a chance on her potential? Maybe go back to school, pursue a passion or start a business? What if she believed it was possible for her to make money and create wealth on her own? What if she believed she could support herself and her daughters without a man? What if she believed in abundance and possibility?

Her life would have gone in a very different direction.

What about you? Do you recognize each of these mindsets in anyone you know? What about within yourself?

We all flip back and forth from one to the other now and then. And sometimes we waver on the line between the two.

Carol Dweck goes into great depth on these two mindsets in her book, *Mindset.* I'm assuming you already know what mindset you are (or you're teetering back and forth between the two) and that's why you're here. You want to adopt the mindset of growth, abundance, and possibility, right? So instead of elaborating on the individual mindsets themselves, we're going to cover, in depth, what causes us to think the way we do. And then go even deeper into how to flip the switch and achieve your goals, dreams, and desires with ease. Because here's the bottom line: It's a choice!

You want to be more open. To be more in tune with the possibilities that exist for you. You want a more abundant life. You want financial freedom. And you want to embrace all that awaits you when you learn how to kick your limiting beliefs to the curb and take charge of what you want. It's possible. And it starts right here and now.

Are you ready to flip the switch on your mindset? Awesome! Let's get to it.

You will attract into your life that in which you choose to focus on.

# Chapter 3
## Why Mindset Matters

What causes us to think the way we do? And why does managing your mindset matter so much? Why is it so important to flip the switch from a limited (negative) mindset to a growth (positive) mindset? The short answer is: your mindset determines how you interact with the world around you and therefore is what creates your reality.

The longer answer has a lot more to do with brain science, choices, and the Universal Laws.

Often, we focus most of our time and energy on what is instead of what could be. Some people call that reality, but it's only one version of reality. The truth is that both, our desires (everything we do want), and our fears (everything we don't want), are equal possibilities. And what our focus does, is tip the scale in one direction or the other—either toward our desires or away from them.

I've spent years studying the power of the mind, and the culmination of all my research agrees on this: The power to shift our reality lies in the ability to shift our focus. This phenomenon is explained by the universal Law of Attraction (LOA) and Law of Vibration (LOV), as well as basic brain science. The Law of

Attraction says that "you will attract into your life that in which you choose to focus on." So basically, the thoughts we think, turn into the things that manifest in our life. How often has something suddenly appeared in your life that caused you to say, *"Wow! I was just thinking about you/that/him the other day?"* Some will say that's a coincidence, but LOA says those coincidences will show up in your life because you thought them into existence. The Law of Attraction demonstrates the result of our mental focus.

Similarly, the Law of Vibration has strong roots in quantum physics (though I won't go too Einstein on you). Mainly, the Law of Vibration is based on the idea that everything is made up of energy in its purest form. Everything has a vibration—you, me, the chair you're sitting in, a cheeseburger, your favorite sweater, and most importantly, emotions. What the LOV explicitly states is that when it comes to vibration, like attracts like. Our personal vibration is created and maintained by our internal emotions. And we will attract things, people, and ideas that match that same vibration. So our feelings dictate our vibrational frequency, and then we attract other things that are of that same frequency.

Brain science says that we have the power to change our reality by simply changing our conscious thoughts. This concept is based on the scientific understanding of how neural networks are created and can be summed up with the phrase, "neurons that fire together, wire together" coined by neuropsychologist, Donald Hebb. When I first started learning about how the brain works, I heard that statement over and over, but I had no idea what it meant. I had to look it up and figure it out. So rather than have you running off on a YouTube frenzy trying to figure out what in the world I'm talking about, here is a crash course.

Our brain is the boss. It tells our bodies what to do. It controls everything—our breathing, our memories, our thoughts, our feelings, and our behaviors. But how does the brain know what to do? The brain gets its commands from the neurons within it. Neurons are like tiny little soldiers hard at work in the brain. But alone, they are not useful. They work in teams. When one neuron sends a message to another neuron, a neural pathway (or communication signal) is formed. It is this neural pathway itself that contains the power. This pathway tells the brain what action to take—what to think, what to remember, how to move, and how to react. Everything the body does, starts with a signal in the brain.

The more two neurons communicate the same signal to each other, the stronger the pathway (or pattern) becomes. A pattern becomes subconscious when, with enough repetition, the brain no longer needs to process the information it's receiving consciously. Instead, the action or response to the information it's receiving becomes automatic or subconscious. This is how habits are formed. The more we do it, the less we have to think about it, and the easier it becomes. That's because we're forming strong neural pathways that make the action easier and, over time, automatic.

So how does this affect you? Well, if you can train the neural pathways in your brain to signal the body (your thoughts, feelings, and behaviors) to only engage in actions that result in you getting the life you want, wouldn't that be pretty powerful?

I'm happy to inform you, you absolutely can! And that's what we're going to do together!

Here's how it works: When we think a particular thought (one neuron sends a signal to another neuron), a neural pathway is formed that signals the brain to release chemicals into our nervous system that tell our body how to feel. Those feelings then cause our bodies to release more chemicals that then affect our thoughts, which (you guessed it!), releases more brain chemicals that reinforce and strengthen our feelings. And the cycle repeats. Good or bad, it all starts with that original thought.

*Let me show you how this can play out:*

Lately, you've been thinking a lot about purchasing a new home (focus). You need to make more money, yet every time the thought pops into your mind, you are overcome by a wave of anxiety and worry (vibration) about how you'll ever be able to pay off your debt and afford to upgrade your home. What happens next just confirms what you've been thinking and feeling:

> **Trigger:** You come home, and your mailbox is full of bills.
>
> This trigger creates the **thought**: *"I'm up to my ears in debt. It's going to take forever to pay this off. I'm so broke."*
>
> Which then causes a release of chemicals in your brain that evoke **feelings** of impatience and frustration.
>
> From that place of impatience and frustration, you begin to **think:** "I don't get it; how come everyone else can afford their dream home? I want to be rich! I work so hard. Why does this have to be so difficult!?"
>
> These thoughts cause a release of chemicals in the brain that causes you to **feel** burnt-out and overwhelmed.
>
> From this place of feeling burnt-out and overwhelmed, you **think** to yourself: *"It's not fair! Why do some people have it so easy? Like Susie, money just falls into her lap. Why does she have so much money? She doesn't even use it wisely!"*

Which then causes a release of more chemicals that create **feelings** of resentfulness and anger.

Which then send you on a **thought** tangent of: *"That's not my style; I'll never be like that. It doesn't matter anyway because I'll probably be in debt for rest of my life and I'll never be able to afford to move."*

This thought tangent causes a release of even more chemicals that leave you **feeling** defeated, victimized, disempowered, and unworthy.

Woah! That went downhill fast, huh? I know you've experienced this. Heck! You may have even gone through it today when you checked the mail! When you look at examples like this, you can see how closely our thoughts and emotions are connected and rely on one another for survival.

Of course, that result of focusing on something negative doesn't always have to mean an emotional downward spiral. It can also cause the formation of giant blind spots—which can be just as detrimental. Those blind spots are the reason you can only see what is right in front of you instead of imagining what *could* be right in front of you, and therefore bringing that possibility into focus and into your reality.

Here's an example of a blind spot I recently experienced when shopping for dining room chairs. I had seen the perfect upholstered chairs on Pinterest and was determined to find those exact ones. Because of my Type-A, hyper-organized personality, I created an alphabetical list of manufacturers and stores that I needed to contact or visit in search of these chairs. I started at the top of my list and began physically visiting stores and websites until I finally found them in "H." (I'm not kidding, not a single manufacturer from A-G even had anything close!) But, then I realized the dimensions were all wrong. They were too wide and wouldn't fit. I felt defeated and totally bummed out. I had to start over. So, of course, back to Pinterest I went! (Where else, right?)

I saw a beautiful dining room with . . . wooden chairs. "*Huh,*" I thought. "*Wooden chairs?*" I hadn't thought of *wooden* chairs. I mean, I knew wooden chairs existed, I just hadn't considered them as a possibility for the look I was going for. "*Interesting.*" So I went back to the alphabetical list I created, fully prepared to restart the grueling search. And what I found was that every single store on my list had at least one version of *that* style chair! But I hadn't noticed it before because I was so focused on finding those perfect upholstered chairs. Once I became aware of the wooden chairs (Boom!) they were everywhere! I was suddenly abundant in chair options!

Most people have experienced this with a car, an outfit, or a pair of shoes. Once you become aware of something, you suddenly begin to notice it everywhere! Does that mean it wasn't there before? Of course not. It was always there. It's just that before you labeled it as "important" by choosing to focus on it, your brain was labeling it as "unimportant" and filtering it out of your awareness.

That's how the Law of Attraction works. In this instance, it was chairs. For you, it will be something entirely different, but the concept remains the same—you bring into your reality (or awareness) that in which you choose to focus on.

The trick is to maintain your focus on that which you desire, and not limit your imagination based on your current circumstances and what seems within the realm of possibility at the moment. Just because we are aware that something is possible, doesn't necessarily mean that we believe that we can have it. If we truly want to believe that our wildest dreams are possible for us, we have to train our brain to find proof that supports that belief. It has been said that the human brain processes 400 billion bits of information every single second. Its job is to filter out all of the information that doesn't seem to apply to us and is, therefore, deemed unimportant. But you can choose what applies to you. You have the power to tell your brain what's important. So if you want to find proof that something is possible, all you have to do is shift your focus and start looking for it.

Think about what happens when you're watching reruns of your favorite TV show. Even though you've seen it a dozen times before, you're captivated until a commercial comes on, right? And for the next three minutes you completely zone out and start thinking about all the things you have to do the next day—grocery shop, pick up your dry cleaning, call your mom back—and you're not paying any attention to what's on the screen.

Then, Thursday rolls around, and you meet a few friends for happy hour. They say, "*Have you seen that commercial with the talking dog? It's hilarious!*" You search your memory bank and . . . nothing. No recollection of that commercial at all. Clearly, it's not on the channel you watch.

Then, that night, you go home, turn on *The Big Bang Theory* (just like you do every night) and bam! What do you see? The first commercial that comes on is the talking dog commercial. You laugh. And then you ask yourself, *Wow! How many times has this commercial come on? And why haven't I noticed it before?*

Here's the answer: Because it wasn't important. It held no value for you until your friends told you how funny it was. Now, because it contains meaning (connection to your friends and laughter), it holds value. You desired a laugh, so you, without realizing it, instructed your brain to watch out for it, so, that's what it did.

The brain tackles a lot of information on a regular basis, and to avoid total burnout and overwhelm, it has developed systems for keeping things manageable. It has learned to tune out anything that seems unimportant and notice only the things that have been labeled, by you, as important.

Of course, teaching your brain to relabel what's important takes practice. Our brains love patterns and routines. The more you maintain a focus on what you desire, the more you work that "focus muscle" and the easier it becomes for your brain to notice the bits of information around you that supports that desire.

In the case above, if what you desire is a good laugh, and the more you focus your attention and *look* for things that make you laugh, the more you'll find them. Your brain will begin to look for things that it thinks you'll find funny and labels those things as important enough to get your attention. And the more you see something funny and pause to enjoy it, the more your brain thinks, *"Yes, that's good. Keep doing that!"* And because your brain is now programmed to notice funny things, your life is becomes filled with joy and laughter.

Training your brain to focus on what is desired rather than what is automatic requires conscious attention. For instance, think about your routine drive home from work (or school, or the grocery store). You've driven this route so often that you drive it on autopilot. Your body knows when to turn on the blinker, when to merge and when to turn. It's automatic. But what if you have to make a stop before heading home that requires you to take a different route? Now that you have a new desired destination, you have to consciously *focus* on that destination, so your mind and body don't click back into autopilot. Without focus, you'll miss your turn and end up back at home, like every other day.

That's how brain patterns work. When we aren't focused on *interrupting the pattern*, by consciously changing our focus, we continue to do the same thing our brains have been programmed to do. We continuously end up in the same place, getting the same results. And I'm assuming that's not where you want to be anymore.

I get that it can be difficult to imagine what possibilities are out there or which ones are available to you. (Spoiler alert: there are limitless possibilities out there, and they're ALL available to you!) To discover them, however, you must first open yourself up to the idea of limitless possibilities as a concept. You don't need to see the exact possibilities or the specifics, in fact, trying to figure out the logistics can block you even more. Instead, just open yourself to the idea of new possibilities.

Here's a beautiful story about how my client, Lizzy, did just that:

> On our five-year anniversary, my husband and I headed from our hometown in Pennsylvania to Colorado to go hiking. We love our long hikes because it gives us a chance to reconnect with nature and each other. While walking and talking, our conversation turned into us discussing how much we loved being surrounded by nature and in a community where nature was an integral part of everyday life. Pennsylvania is cold for a good chunk of the year, and during those months we tend to spend more time indoors than out.
>
> It was at that moment—hiking in nature and

connecting with each other—that we opened ourselves up to the possibility of living somewhere other than the east coast. We discussed what would be important to us if we were to entertain moving. We discussed living in a region and community where food was viewed as fuel, and there was a focus on health and sustainability. We talked about surrounding ourselves with people who are driven to make an impact in the world. And we talked about how magical it would be to live where the outdoors could be enjoyed year-round. Then we forgot all about the conversation and enjoyed the rest our anniversary trip together.

Six weeks after returning home, my husband received a job offer from a company that is built on a founding mission of ending poverty through organic agriculture in Sonoma County, California, where it's sunny year-round and most of the day is spent outdoors.

We went on another long hike through the woods, this time near our home, to discuss our thoughts about moving across the country, away from our families and everything we've ever known. While we were deep in our conversation of "Should we? Or shouldn't we?" a mourning dove feather appeared at my husband's feet. A mourning dove, if you believe in Universal Signs, is a symbol of hope and peace. And when a mourning dove feather finds you, it's a reminder to let go of the turmoil within, remain open-hearted and turn your thoughts to joy. It is a reminder that this time of transition shall soon pass and peace will follow.

We accepted it as a clear sign that we needed to surrender ourselves to the wind, go to new heights (even if they are scary), remain peaceful and calm and trust that the transition will be comfortable and for the best.

The feather, for us, confirmed that our wild dream of living somewhere that fit all of our dream location requirements was not so far-fetched after all and was possible.

I'm happy to say, we've been living in California several months now, and we love it. It's incredible what can happen when you simply open yourself up to new possibilities.

When we are closed-minded and pretend to know what is (and what is not) possible for us, what we're really doing is building walls that keep us contained within the reality that is familiar to us. We are creating our own limitations. By opening yourself up to all possibilities, the answers find their way to you—like me with my chairs, and Lizzy moving across the country. When you embrace what's possible, your thoughts switch from scarcity, fear, and doubt, to abundance, curiosity, and certainty. Those thoughts evoke feelings of excitement, joy, love, freedom, and fulfillment.

You don't have to know the answers or have a plan. You don't even have to know how the possibilities will manifest. You just have to open yourself up and focus on your desire (whether it's a desire to laugh, a desire for a completed dining room set, a desire to immerse yourself in nature, or something else entirely). When you become aware of what you want and allow yourself to be open to how it might come to you, anything is possible.

# Chapter 4
## Identifying Your Triggers

If you finished the last chapter wondering, *"How in the world am I supposed to just 'open myself up' to the idea of new possibilities?! How do I do that? I don't have the first clue where to start. And wait, why is it so freakin' hard to even conceptualize that? What's wrong with me!?"*

Let me assure you, nothing is wrong with you. It's just your brain rebelling against something new. It's just trying to keep you safe within your limits of familiarity. Listen, our experiences have conditioned us to believe what we currently believe, and to focus on what we currently focus on. Everything our brain knows is a result of our experiences and choices up until now. That's what we're all working with. But we can choose to think and live outside of those limits if we want to. That is a choice that is always available to us.

Without understanding that we do, in fact, hold the power to choose, and without making a conscious effort to see beyond our own limits, we are subject to inheriting the behaviors, thought patterns, and responses of those around us. We watch, we learn, we emulate.

We typically associate learning with reading books, attending classes and taking notes. But so much of what we learn is simply observation and modeling. This started waaaaay back before you can even remember.

Think about the last time you played with a baby. You probably made some silly faces, stuck your tongue out, opened up your mouth super wide and made popping noises with your mouth. And then you watched as the baby began trying to mimic you and make the same faces back at you. And when they succeed, you clapped and celebrated, right? And just like that—boom!—a connection is made. A neural pathway is created in that baby's brain. The same thing happens when we teach babies to eat. We put smashed-up food on a spoon, show them the spoon, and then open our own mouth wide so that they will do the same long enough for us to shove the smashed peas in there. And after a yummy meal of peas (and maybe some applesauce), another neural pathway is formed. After a few meals, it's a strong, solidified pattern. It becomes one of those things that baby doesn't have to focus on anymore. It becomes a habit. See spoon, open mouth, eat food. Repeat. That's how you learned, too, and now, when you sit down to eat, you don't have to consciously think about what to do. It's automatic.

We do the same thing with the rest of our world, too. As young children, as teens, and even as adults. We watch the world around us. We pay attention to what's going on and how people around us are acting and reacting. And we emulate it. We watch the people around us, and we use their words, we think similarly, we learn how to behave in various situations, and interact with the world around us by modeling the people around us. And after a while, these words, thoughts, and behaviors become subconscious patterns, and we no longer have to watch, learn, and emulate. We just "do" without thinking or trying.

Although, as adults, we are constantly learning new things,

most of our subconscious patterns were formed before we were seven years old. It happens super early on. So if you'd like, you can go ahead and blame your childhood environment for all the negative thought patterns and limiting beliefs that you picked up in your formative years. Go ahead and take a minute; do what you must to experience the anger, frustration, and blame about how your parents (or caregivers) raised you. Then come back and acknowledge that you are now an adult and you have a choice. You can blame everyone who had a hand in raising you for how your life has turned out, or you get to take control of your future by doing something about it right now. Let me say that again:

**The choices you make today will determine the quality of your future. You can choose a bright future or a dim one. Either way, you're in control.**

How's that for empowering?

Choosing to take that control of your future is a powerful step. But it would be false for me to claim that choosing to take control is the end of the story. It's only the beginning. Going forward, you're going to have to maintain that sense of control and empowerment. You're going to have to resist the temptation to go back to your old ways. And you're going to have to work to keep the negativity out so you can focus on the positivity and possibility that awaits you at every turn.

You must become aware and critical of your environment, and of everything around you and how it is contributing to your current mindset. What are you letting influence you? What do you need to avoid or let go of to stop it from negatively affecting your life?

There is potentially a lot that has been influencing your mindset. Everything from the way you feel when you drive through your neighborhood to the decor in your house to the people around you to the media you consume. It's going to take some time to assess all of it. Once you start paying attention, you'll get a pretty good idea of what's helping you move forward and what's keeping you stuck.

Let's take a look at how some factors may be influencing or triggering you.

## People in your inner circle

**Reverters:** These are the people that keep you stuck in old patterns that no longer serve you. You're a little more mature and mindful of your choices these days; you don't do shots anymore and no longer stay out until 4 a.m. on the weekends. But the second you get around your rockstar beer-bongin', f-bombin' old crowd, you suddenly feel compelled to drink more than your body weight in liquor, whip out the old slang and do something regrettably stupid. In sixth grade, we called it peer pressure, but as an adult, it's the allowance of re-emerging patterns that we thought we had outgrown. Oh, the power of influence. We often allow these reverters to influence our language, thoughts, and feelings.

There are also the Debbie Downer kind of reverters. You know the ones, when you're in a really good place, but an hour with them makes you see all the negative parts of your life. Your work is going great, you're in a good relationship, and you have an awesome vacation coming up. Then, you go out for a night on the town with a group of friends who complain about every. Last. Thing. In less than an hour, you go from being on the Gratitude Train to complaining about how annoying your spouse is, how ungrateful your kids are and what a jerk your boss is. Before going out with these friends, you saw your life as close to perfect. Now, you're fantasizing about what life would be like if you'd never have gotten married, or had kids, or taken that stupid job. It's pretty amazing how your focus can shift like that, isn't it? I mean, every situation and relationship has its pros and cons and ups and downs, but it's up to you to choose what you focus on. **Ask yourself:** *"Are the people in my life triggering me to focus on the positives or negatives?"*

**Energy vampires**: These folks are a special kind of annoying. They are the ones that suck the energy out of your day, or your life, depending on how often you're around them. Literally, talking to them for five minutes on the phone can be draining. They're the ones that call you again and again for advice on the same exact subject. (Their inconsiderate boss, their toxic relationship, their meddling mother-in-law.) They love being miserable and prefer to stay that way as long as they can find an audience willing to listen. They know that they have the option to do something about their situation (like taking your brilliant advice), but they choose not to. They've been operating this way for so long that the thought of choosing a new path, means stepping out of their zone of familiarity, which is just too hard and scary.

**Victims:** The victims in our lives are the hardest to distance ourselves from because we feel bad for them. It's easy to get caught up in wanting to help them out, especially because it makes us feel like we're doing them a service. But here's the thing: you can't help those who refuse to help themselves. And victims are not interested in helping themselves because they don't believe that it's possible for them to change their situation. They don't even believe they have a choice in the matter. Their reality is a result of external circumstances beyond their control. Setbacks and disasters happen *to* them, not *for* them. They refuse to find the lesson or the blessing in situations and instead feel as though the world is conspiring against them, almost as if to punish them. Seeing someone else do well or succeed is just one more form of punishment—rubbing it in their face that that will never happen for them. And let me tell you, these folks good at laying on the guilt trip! I know it's tempting to feel like we can help them, but what really ends up happening, is they suck your energy, drain your mental focus and pull your happy thoughts and high vibes down to their level until you're in their pessimistic underground. Blech. No bueno, amigo.

**Negative Protectors:** These people are dream sabotagers disguised as concerned loved ones. They genuinely believe that their advice is helping you by keeping you out of harm's way. But the walls they've built up to keep themselves safe inside their own familiarity zone are so thick that they cannot see any possibilities that exist outside of it—for themselves, or for you.

So, when you mention your plans to step outside of those walls, into the great unknown to pursue your dreams, they warn you of the risks, the consequences, *everything* that could potentially go wrong. Their well-meaning advice is actually coming from a place of fear. The fear that keeps them from pursuing their own dreams is the same fear they feel for you. While they mean well, their projected fear has the potential to deplete all of your positive energy and send you down a rabbit hole of negative thoughts and fears, too.

## News stories & Social Media

The news and information on social media you choose to consume can also dramatically affect your energy and perspective. The news can be a real drag—murder, arson, kidnapping, shooting. I mean, have you ever watched the news and walked away thinking, *"Wow! That really made me feel positive and happy?"*

Generally speaking, watching the news is depressing and awful. That's because the media chooses to focus on the negative aspects of the world. There have been studies done that show that the more you watch the news, the more anxious and depressed you become. That's because when you watch the news and focus your awareness on the horrible things that are happening, perhaps right in your neighborhood, it's easy to start to believe the world is a cruel and scary place.

Social media is another place to beware of negativity. But this one can be trickier. Software algorithms are designed to learn what you like and respond accordingly. So if you engage and "like" a lot of positive posts, the algorithm responds by showing your more happy stories and positive people.

After a while, it starts to feel like everyone has a picture-perfect life and five minutes on Facebook leaves you feeling like there is something terribly wrong with your own life. People don't post what's "real," they only post what they're proud of. Even though we sort of know that it's everyone's highlight reel, we still end up comparing ourselves.

Likewise, if the algorithms notice that we engage and interact to negatively charged rants and posts, they respond by showing us more of those. Before we know it, a simple check-in on social media can leave us feeling angry, lonely, empty, and depressed.

## Physical environment

There's a reason we spend time browsing Pinterest, Houzz, and Zillow or driving around looking at beautiful homes. When you find one you love, you stop and linger on it for a couple of minutes, fantasizing about what it's like to live in such beauty. Have you ever imagined yourself living in your picture-perfect dream home and then, when the daydream was over, took a good look at your own less-than-ideal home and felt resentful, angry, hopeless or discouraged?

Look around you right now. Do the things you see make you happy? How would you describe your surroundings? Do they light you up and bring you joy? Do you enjoy spending time in your kitchen? Do you love cuddling up on your couch? Do the things around you nurture your spirit? Or are they screaming for a makeover?

If your surroundings don't make you happy and bring you warm fuzzy feelings of joy, why is that? How do you justify not living in an environment full of items that make you happy when you see them? *"The kids need things. They come first" "It costs money to replace it, and since it still works, it would be wasteful to get rid of it."*

Honey, that is a damn cop out! You deserve to love everything in your environment. You are already worthy of that. You don't have to wait. You really don't. Your environment emulates your sense of worth. It is a reflection of how you feel about yourself. If you are surrounded by things that make you happy, it's like you're saying to the Universe, "I'm worth it." If you're not saying that right now, it's time for an upgrade!

## Entertainment: (books/TV/movies/music)

If you spend enough time consuming certain messages in the media, you start to think and act as if the world is just like that. Someone who listens to nothing but gangster rap is likely to have their mind on their money, and money on their mind. (Yes, I listen to rap!) They are more likely to perceive the world as a place where hustle is necessary and place high value on name-brand material possessions and are on a constant mission to acquire more. Someone who listens to nothing but country music (which I also listen to) is more likely to take pride in the simple things in life—a home cooked meal, a relaxing Sunday afternoon with family, a loving relationship.

I can't help but think that reality television has influenced the behaviors of lots of people in the last decade, as well. Do people really have that much drama in their lives? Think about the TV shows and movies you watch, the books you read, and the music you listen to. What do they make you think about? Do they encourage you to think about what's possible in this life? Or do they make you think your current life is inadequate or that you should expect drama from all of your friends?

A more important question: what do you want the media you consume to make you think about? Because here's the point, we emulate too. It's not just kiddos. We watch and imitate. What we put into our brains is what it will spit back out.

It's clear how these triggers affect your energy and life perspective. Don't get overwhelmed though. Yes, you do have to set some boundaries and start shielding your energy a bit. But this is all under your control once you learn how to manage it. When it is possible to minimize your exposure to triggers and create energetic boundaries, you absolutely should. But when you can't eliminate the trigger, what you *can* do is teach yourself to respond differently—in a way that is healthy and serves you better. You can reprogram how your brain is conditioned to react.

Here's a short priority list:

1. Minimize triggers in your environment
2. Change the way you react to your triggers

Boom. Life-changers, y'all!

Awareness of what is damaging your focus and energy is transformative. It's the first and most impactful step in this process.

Now, remember, our brains are creatures of habit. Eliminating triggers and responding differently might sound great to you right now, but be prepared, your brain is going to resist. It's just what it's designed to do.

Reinforcement is the comfy, fluffy blanket of the brain. Whenever we do anything, the result of that action becomes a reason in our brain to either keep doing it or to never do it again. When the same result happens over and over, it becomes a conditioned response and therefore predictable. Brains looooove predictability. Predictability adds fuzzy slippers to the blanket. And when your brain gets that comfy, it's hard to ask it to change. I mean, when you're on the couch watching Netflix with your comfy blanket and warm slippers, do you want to get up and do something risky? Um, no. Because snuggling up on the couch isn't going to magically transform your life.

You know that job that you show up to every day but don't like? You probably dream of more money and a workplace where the people you work with appreciate and respect you and your ideas. Where you are valued, and they shower you with extra money and extend your vacation time as a reward for your valuable contribution.

But your reality? They don't respect you; you don't have nearly enough time off, you're overworked and underpaid. And yet you still keep going.

WHY?

Because you've been reinforcing to your brain, for awhile now, that this is the way the world works. Reinforcing the belief that, *"I'm not the only one." "Most people don't love their job." "I have to work hard to earn a promotion if I want more money." "This is as good as it gets."* Reinforcement, is the brain's favorite slippers. I mean, they're smelly and old at this point, but it's just easier to keep wearing them than to go out and get new ones, right?

Experience tells you that if you continue to go to this job, it will mean a predictable, conditioned result: a steady paycheck. You could rock the boat and quit your job to start a business, but that's unpredictable. And when you let your thoughts wander there, they begin to spiral into something like this:

> *What if it doesn't work??*
> *What if I fail?*
> *What if I end up with no money because the business isn't profitable?*
> *What about health insurance?*
> *What if I have to go to the hospital?*
> *The medical bills will kill me.*
> *I'll lose my house.*
> *Where will I live?*
> *I'd have to go live in someone's basement or find a cheap apartment.*
> *That would be the worst thing ever.*
> *How shameful and embarrassing.*
> *I'd have to explain to everyone that I f-ed up and that's why I'm now living in my best friends' basement.*

And on the spiral continues. You feel an onslaught of nervousness, anxiety, doubt, and exhaustion from just thinking about it. Your brain wins. You don't take the chance. You do what's comfortable (but kind of sucks) instead of what's desirable. Why? Because your past programming and patterns have told you it's effective. It gets you to the goal that gets you by. But it's not expansive. It's restrictive.

How often do you make unpleasant decisions just because it gets you to a goal that is a warped definition of success? A goal that you've defined "good enough" for now?

Kids do this all the time. A child will throw a temper tantrum on the floor until her mom bribes her with candy to behave. The goal was candy. The means to get it was a tantrum. Though unpleasant, it worked; therefore, it was effective. Are there better (less upsetting) ways to get candy? Sure. But why go through the trouble of finding a new way when this way already works?

It's a silly example, but in all honesty, we're doing the same thing as adults. We're settling for good enough when we could (and should) be seeking out something extraordinary. Don't you think it's about time to find a better way to get the "candy"?

We resist changing our behavior and searching for new, better ways, to achieve our desired outcome because we are operating in a limited mindset with the belief that "it is what it is" and this is the only way.

That's not true, though. There is a better way. We can choose to replace negative thoughts with positive ones, which in turn will create empowering feelings within us that help us to take action toward getting the things we want. The result is that we expand into a world of possibilities rather than remain restricted in our self-imposed world of limitations.

When we switch our mindset by interrupting the old patterns of unwanted thoughts, feelings, and behaviors, and replacing them with thoughts, feelings, and behaviors that are in alignment with who we truly are at our core, we begin to change the way we see ourselves and the world around us.

My client, Tiffany, recently had a mindset switch moment while attending a seminar with best-selling author and marketing guru, Michael Port. She was one of six lucky VIP members to be brought on stage for one-to-one coaching with Michael. He asked her what she did for a living, and she went into a story about how she's a chef but attached the disclaimer that she received her degree online. He noticed (and likely felt) the odd vibe around her and called her out—in front of 600 people! *"Why are you telling me you got your degree online? Why would I care about that?"* he asked her.

Tiffany explained that "real" chefs wouldn't consider her to be as valuable because she wasn't classically trained in a brick and mortar culinary school where they teach both culinary arts and the business skills required to open and operate a restaurant. Since she was already an experienced marketer and had a pretty solid business foundation, she didn't feel she needed the business part.

But because in her world, real chefs went to "real" culinary academies, she wasn't allowing herself to own her status as a chef. She was shying away from marketing her business and confidently telling people who she was and what she did. She felt like a fraud. A feeling that lingered until that day on stage when Michael called her out. He, very publicly, interrupted her negative thought pattern by challenging her to think differently about her skills when he asked, *"Do you have the skills of a traditionally trained chef? Did you learn to cook at this online school?"*

At that moment, Tiffany realized that she had all the same skills as any other chef. It was her past programming that was sabotaging her and keeping her playing small and safe. She says,

"*I realized that when I have confidence in myself, people have confidence in me. I went from resisting marketing myself for fear that someone would find out I wasn't classically trained to telling everyone who'll listen what I do and why I'm so passionate about it. I stopped doubting my abilities and stepped into my role as a real chef. And it felt amazing!*"

Tiffany's *Kids Cooking School* is now booming, and her students are thriving beyond belief—some have even been considered for national cooking shows!

All of this wouldn't have been possible if she hadn't interrupted the negative pattern and embraced new ways of thinking about herself.

We all have the opportunity to change the way we think about ourselves and what's possible for us. All we have to do is decide. When we stop settling for "good enough" and decide to think about ourselves in new, positive ways, we are in essence telling the Universe, "*I believe in myself, and I will not settle for less than I desire. I am worth it. I am enough. I am ready for the next step!*"

# Chapter 5
## Flip the Switch!

Once you take the time to acknowledge the hang-ups and brain patterns that are contributing to your current reality, you get to make a choice—a better choice—to start getting the results (and the life) you want.

You get to shift from "life happens to me" to "life happens because of me!"

But you can only get there when you claim responsibility. Listen, the way you feel about your life, and everything in it, is a result of your choices, actions, and beliefs. And if you're reading this book, there's something (or maybe several things) going on in your life that you'd like to change.

I get that you can't control every little thing around you. Situations will arise that are beyond your immediate control. You will experience events like death, illness, accidents, and setbacks. While you can't necessarily control or prevent those situations from happening, what you can control is how you react to them. You can choose the mindset you want to operate from. You can choose the limited mindset and play the victim, pretending as if you don't have a choice at all, or you can choose the growth mindset and see it as an opportunity to learn and grow. I'm not saying that everything will always be sunshine and rainbows. What I am saying, though, is that you get to choose the meaning you give to each situation and how you let it affect you.

What are the aspects of your life that aren't serving you anymore? Whether it's your job, your business, your health, your body, your relationships, or something else, it's time to be honest with yourself, and know that it's happening because of you.

That might sound harsh, but I invite you to try to see it as an opportunity instead of a judgment. Because really, that's what it is. It's an invitation to choose something different.

You are in complete control of your experience. If you want a to build a profitable business, travel, look good naked, wake up next to your soulmate every morning, or change the world, all you have to do is believe that it's possible for you. And I'm going to teach you how to do that in a way that's super simple; it's just a matter of working through the mindset layers, one at a time, and replacing the words, thoughts, feelings, and beliefs that don't support your desire, with ones that do. Easy peasy.

If you've ever been in therapy, you were probably encouraged to search your memories and find the root of the problem, which is likely connected to your upbringing. And for many of us, that's true, and important to acknowledge.

But that's not what I'm going to ask you to do.

The power to create your future doesn't lie in the past. It resides in the here and now. It is not the responsibility of your parents' or your partner. It's your responsibility and yours alone.

At this point in your life, you have two choices:

1. Continue to blame other people and ignore the fact that you have the power to choose a new path for yourself and create the life you really want, or

2. Create and implement a new (much better) belief system.

Let's take a minute to go down the rabbit hole of option #1. We'll call it "The Easy Option." Say you continue as you've been living. You put this book down and never follow through with anything you've learned here. You continue to make the same decisions and get the same results. What does your life look like in five years from now? What about ten years? Twenty years?

Your life is basically the same as it is now, right? You have the same career. You're making the same amount of money. Living in the same place. Driving the same kind of car. Spending time with the same people. Having the same conversations. Fighting the same fights.

I mean, I don't know your specifics, but I imagine when you picture your future as being pretty much the same as it is now, you get a gut-wrenching feeling in the pit of your stomach. I imagine you're ready for more—a whole lot more.

I can still remember my own gut-wrenching feeling the first time I asked myself those same questions. My husband and I had just left a house-warming party at our friend's custom-built, mini-mansion, and were driving back to our "5-year starter home" that we were still living in—12 years later. Our friends were the same age as us, yet they were doing so much better, financially. And I remember thinking, *"Why are they doing so well, while we're over here living paycheck to paycheck, struggling to survive?"*

Then the answer hit me. **They made better choices.**

That's it. It was that simple. They chose what they wanted, and they got it.

Then, I asked myself what would happen if we each continued down our current paths. I realized that in five, ten, or twenty years, our friends would be consistently upgrading. Nicer homes, luxurious vacations, fancy cars. They'd be able to send their kids to college and pay for their weddings. And if we continued on our current path, we'd still be exactly where we were, trying desperately to make ends meet.

I instantly had images of the many people I know—family, friends, and neighbors—flash through my mind. All the people who had passed retirement age and were still working themselves to the bone, simply because they chose to remain a victim to their limiting beliefs. They didn't realize or accept that they had the power to choose a new (better) path. I knew that I didn't want to be like them. I wanted to be like our friends. I knew something had to change. I knew I had to make a different choice. That was eight years ago. And let me tell you, that choice paid off big time! I am now operating a business that fills me with love, joy, and gratitude every day; I'm living in my dream home, driving a brand-new luxury vehicle. My kids have a college fund, and money isn't a struggle, but rather a tool that offers me an abundance of choices. It's pretty magical!

Eight years ago, I was working as a coat check girl at a club in Detroit. If you had given me a thousand chances to guess what my life would look like today, I wouldn't have been able to do it. That's because if I had tried to make a prediction about my future based on what my life looked like in that moment, I would have ended up limiting myself to what was probable rather than what was possible.

What does your future hold for you? Try not to get stuck

thinking about what is probable. Instead, imagine what could be possible. In a perfect world, what do you desire to be, do and have? What would that look like? What would that feel like for you? Give yourself permission to dream up some fabulous details without any further responsibilities or the need to understand how it could happen. Do you dream of traveling the world in style? If so, imagine the way it would feel to fly first class and stay in a luxury resort, eating the finest foods. Or, maybe you desire to be a world-renowned public speaker. If so, what would that feel like for you? Perhaps you dream of having children or starting an animal rescue. Whatever you dream of being, doing or having, know that it is yours the second you decide you want it. All you have to do is open yourself up to the possibility of having it, and then allow it to unfold. That's the simplicity of how the Law of Attraction works.

I'm living an abundant life now because I chose to believe in a dream that was far better than my current circumstance. I chose to believe in myself and open myself up to possibilities. I wanted more. And I decided to get it. I know you want more in your life, too. There is something that isn't serving you anymore. Something you want to change. What is it? Let's take an inventory of those things. Seriously. Awareness of what isn't working is an important step in the process.

*\*\*To get started on this right now, turn to the Discover section of the workbook to complete the Do-Not-Want List exercise.*

Becoming aware of the things that are wrong (or not up to par) in your life, is half the battle. It clues you into the areas that are begging for an upgrade!

So yes, you can take "The Easy Option" and continue doing the same thing over and over and expecting a different result. (Einstein once explained this as the definition of insanity.)

**Or—You. Can. Change. It.**

Let's explore option #2. We'll call this "The (Much) Better Option."

If all of the things you listed on your Do-Not-Want List are a result of your choices, actions, and beliefs (and we both know that they are) all you have to do to get different results is change your choices, actions, and beliefs (your mindset)!

Simple? Yes.

Easy? Eh . . . not at first.

That's because your mindset is like a muscle. It has developed a type of "muscle memory" from running the same patterns for so many years. If you want to create something new, you have to first interrupt the pattern. It's something you have to practice and do over and over again until it becomes habitual.

With practice, though, it eventually becomes easy (and automatic) as it turns into a new pattern. But like I said earlier, brains are lazy. They loooove short cuts. They love to keep you playing small. And they are mostly interested in keeping you safe and as far away from the danger zone as possible. But upgrading your life (by stepping out of your zone of familiarity) to a much more amazing version than it is today isn't life-threatening. Your brain just thinks it is for a little while.

It can be a little like tires in the mud at first. Imagine you live on a dirt road. And every day you drive your truck up and down the same path until your tires begin to create ruts in the road. Over time, you don't even have to steer the truck anymore because your tires will just naturally follow the path (ruts) that are already there.

Your brain works the same way. You've been driving your "Brain Truck" down the same path for so many years now that there is a pattern your brain just follows. It's natural, familiar, and easy.

But the moment you decide to change your pattern and create a new path (a more positive path) things get a little tricky. You have to consciously focus on creating a new path. You have to work to keep your Brain Truck out of those old ruts in the road until a new path has been created. It's going to feel challenging, and possibly even a little scary at times.

But once you start to get intentional about what you choose to focus on, you'll begin to recognize events as they happen, instead of in hindsight. You'll start to think, *"Does this serve me? Where will this lead? Is this really what I want? Am I playing small? Am I capable of more?"* That awareness gives you the power to flip the switch on how you think, feel, and react to your world. It enables you to create circumstances that excite you instead of adding yet another thing to your Do-Not-Want list.

Now let me be super clear here: Stress doesn't stop happening. I wish I had the cure for that, but the fact is, there will always be things that threaten to trigger you into old patterns. You can't eliminate them. Their existence is beyond what you have the power to control.

You can, however, control your response to triggers that threaten to stress you out and pull you back into your old self-defeating ways. Your ability to flip the switch will strengthen the more you continue to focus your attention on the things you do want in your life. So, although triggers will continue to exist, they won't affect you in the same way anymore. They won't drain your energy and drag you down. They'll just bounce off of your new shiny armor of high-vibe energy. You'll react to them in a way that says, "You're a nuisance, but you do not affect me."

My absolute favorite thing that changes, when you upgrade your mindset, is that your "someday" life becomes your "now" reality. You know all the "someday's and one day's" you dream about:

> *Someday I'll buy my dream house.*
> *One of these days I'll start saving for retirement.*
> *Someday we will go on that fantastic family vacation.*
> *One day, maybe, I'll meet the love of my life.*
> *Someday I'll start my business.*
> *One day, maybe, I'll be wealthy.*

When you flip the switch, it's like traveling through time and getting the money, the lover, the dream house—all of it. All of those feelings of freedom, safety, relaxation, and comfort in knowing that everything's fine and there's nothing to stress or worry about. That's what the switch can do for you. No matter where you're at in life right this second.

You can get it all now if you choose to.

Now, if only I could just come and install an actual switch in your brain and call it a day, I would totally do that for you. Unfortunately, that's not how it works. You have to design, build and install your switch yourself. In your own amazing brain. You're the one that controls it.

But don't worry, I've got your back. I have an action plan for you to follow—a system for how you can determine what you need to change and a solid way to implement new patterns into your life today so that all of your tomorrows look infinitely better!

When I said this would take some work, I wasn't kidding. But we're going to take it step by step, layer by layer. We'll work from the outside in. From your surface perceptions to your core beliefs.

It's kind of like a giant Gobstopper. Remember those humongous jawbreaker candies with the colorful flavor layers that you had to suck on foreverrrr to get to the middle?

Your mindset is no different. (Well, it's probably a little less sticky than a half-eaten Gobstopper.) Instead of different flavor layers, you have different mindset layers, in order from the surface to the core they are:

- Words
- Thoughts
- Feelings
- Beliefs

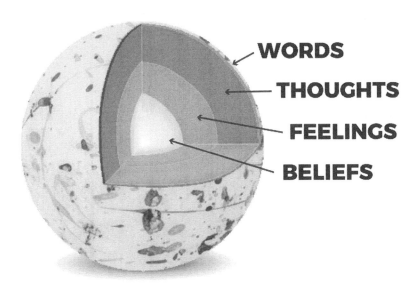

You can't go straight to the core and expect to change your beliefs. I wish it were that simple. But it's not. That would be like asking the U.S. President to change his beliefs about politics or a clergyman to change his religious beliefs. A belief is something that has been solidified in that brain of yours for a long time, maybe even decades. To change the belief, you have to work through the outer layers first. And you can't skip layers, either. Just like you can't get right to the middle of the Gobstopper, you have to work the process, layer by layer, giving your brain the new information and facts it requires to break the old, limiting, patterns, and replace them with new patterns that, when repeated, will solidify into new, empowering, beliefs.

In the next few chapters, we will dive deeper into each layer. We'll figure out what you're doing now, and what your current patterns are. And if those patterns are not serving you, I'll give you some actionable ways to change them so that you can, in effect, create the life you really want.

Sound too good to be true? Well, even if you believe it just a little bit, do yourself a favor and give it a solid try. I think you'll be pleasantly surprised when you realize how mind-blowing and life-altering this mindset work is!

The first layer we will uncover is **Words**. We will figure out what words you're using in your day-to-day lingo and self-talk, in your personal relationships, to describe your financial situation, and we'll discuss how your words affect your overall outlook on life. If you find yourself saying defeating phrases like, *"I can't," "I'm broke," "What is this world coming to?"* or *"I'll never find my soulmate,"* these are some neon-bright clues that you've got some self-limiting beliefs that are keeping you from the life you desire, and could be living right now. The great news is that this is the easiest layer to see, change, and transform.

The second layer we'll tackle is **Thoughts.** Because thoughts are hidden below the surface, they're a little harder to detect. We don't always notice them or share them with others, so you'll need to pay attention to yourself. Your thoughts are the reason you feel the way you do, so understanding them is a necessary gateway to the next layer. Don't worry; I'll make it as easy as possible to work through this layer!

The third layer is **Feelings**. When it comes down to it, how you feel about something is what matters most. Your vision board isn't about the actual car, kitchen or vacation. It's about the way having those things will make you feel. Having the car will make you feel accomplished. The dream kitchen symbolizes your desire to host parties at your home and feel connected to the people whom you invite over. The vacation is a symbol of the freedom that you long for in your life.

I'm going to teach you how to tune into the emotions that fuel your desires and how to use those emotional drivers to choose how you want to feel today and every day for the rest of your life. If you started this chapter feeling heavy, overwhelmed, or nervous about taking full control over your life, no worries. I'll teach you how to let go of those nasty feelings and tap into the emotions that fuel and empower you.

The last and deepest layer we will uncover is **Beliefs**. This layer has veto power over everything that happens in your life. Your beliefs are the gatekeeper of possibility, choosing what to let in and what to keep out. They influence what you think you're capable of and what you feel you deserve. Chances are there are some deep-rooted beliefs that are holding you back. We're going to find out what they are. Then, we're going to change them by working through all the other layers.

Once your beliefs are set up to make success inevitable in your life . . . well, let's just say you're going to need a brand new vision board!

When you get in the habit of noticing, acknowledging, designing, and changing your words, then your thoughts, and then your feelings, the belief itself changes as a result. And the new (better!) belief is solidified. Then the whole thing works in reverse: your new empowering belief causes you to feel better about yourself, which leads to more positive thoughts resulting in more positive words and thus a more positive experience! And then the new cycle continues, and that becomes your new normal.

Remember what I said earlier about you being in complete control? Pretty powerful, right?

These patterns and processes weren't formed overnight though, so they're not going to change overnight. It takes a little the time, energy, and effort. But, trust me, if you're willing to do the work, you'll be doing a happy dance much sooner than you might think!

Are you ready? Let's dive into those layers and start making some dreams come true!

# Chapter 6
## Words Layer

When I was about ten years old, I had a little bit of an attitude. I was a sassy tomboy who thought I was tough because I hung out with all the boys in the neighborhood. I was into Tonka trucks, Hot Wheels, G.I. Joes, and I was the only girl allowed in the Boys Only treehouse. Yep, I was pretty cool.

My best friend, Patrick, lived two doors down from me. He was three years older and a little self-conscious about being overweight. Did that matter in our friendship? Nope. Well, not until the day I used his insecurity as a weapon.

We got into a fight in my front yard. I don't even remember why we were fighting in the first place, but I remember we were yelling at each other and doing our best to spit increasingly offensive insults at one another, as though the person with who came up with the most (and most hurtful) insults would be declared the "winner."

After a few minutes of back-and-forth insults, I looked at him with my eyes all squinty-mad and mustered up all the toughness I had in me and screamed, *"You're so fat, if you stepped on a scale you'd probably break it!"*

And that did it.

He stomped up to me, and placed his (much bigger) hand on my hand, interlaced his fingers with mine, and squeezed while bending my hand backward as if he was threatening to snap my wrist. "Take it back," he demanded. I wouldn't. He kept squeezing harder and harder, but I held my ground and refused to give in. Until finally, my fingers turned blue, the pain became unbearable, and I felt something pop. I screamed. He got scared and ran home. I spent the rest of the afternoon in the hospital being treated for a fractured finger.

Like I said, I had attitude. I'm not proud of that moment. I still feel guilty for flinging those words at him the way I did. But it taught me a valuable lesson: Be mindful of what you say to people. But here's the lesson within the lesson: If Patrick hadn't believed that he was fat, my comment would have bounced right off him like all the other words I flung in his direction that afternoon. But because he did believe it, he allowed that tiny little three-letter word to trigger a nasty feeling within him, and an even nastier reaction. Because of that word (and what it meant to him), he ended up emotionally scarred, and I ended up with a fractured finger.

But it's not the words, themselves, that matter; it's the meaning we give them. The power we allow them to have.

When doing the work to flip the switch, we start with words because they are partially external. Of all the layers, words are the easiest to pay attention to and notice, whether you start listening to your own language or the chatter of those around you. The words you use have a profound connection to the deeper layers, but they can be caught and changed easier than the deeper layers. As I said earlier, there's no point in trying to go right to the belief.

That would be like attempting to run the Boston Marathon

without ever even trying on a pair of running shoes. By starting at the words layer, you're working up to the "big event," strengthening your muscles and stamina, all the while, learning the tools to strengthen your inner game and prepare you for every possible situation—running in adverse weather conditions, leg cramps, fatigue and of course, let's not forget the self-defeating inner dialogue that's stuck on a loop inside your head.

Imagine what would happen if you just showed up at the starting line of the Boston Marathon without ever training to run—not even a single jog around the block. What do you think your brain would do? No doubt it would start with the mental chatter: *"Are you crazy? You can't do this! You've never even run a mile! Remember that time in school when you had to run the mile in gym class, and you came in 19th place, and all your friends made fun of you? This will be just like that! But in front of millions of people. What if you fall? What if you pass out?"*

Just like training for a marathon, working toward any goal in baby steps improves confidence, prepares you for those less-than-ideal situations, and reinforces the belief that it is possible! Your brain prefers it that way. By starting at the words layer, you're taking the first step toward conditioning (or training) your brain to accept a new belief. Doing this takes time. Just like it would be nearly impossible to go from being a couch potato to running a marathon; it's just as difficult to go from believing you'll be poor for the rest of your life (or you'll never find your soulmate, or never lose weight, or whatever) to believing that wealth (or a hot lover or a six-pack of abs) is waiting for you right around the corner. You can't just say to your brain: *"Believe this now"* and expect it to work. Your brain needs more of a reason than that. The logical part of you needs proof that what you'd like it to believe is actually possible. And this is done by consciously seeking out information that supports your desired belief.

Here's an example of how repeated exposure to a message can change what we inherently believe, using milk as the subject. This is an example of how repeated messaging can change the way you think and feel about anything—yourself, money, relationships, business, and yes, even milk.

If you grew up in the 1980s, you probably believed that "Milk does a body good," right? For the most part, that was considered gospel. Milk was served in schools and parents wouldn't excuse their children from the dinner table until they drank all their milk. That is, until the 2000s when media started to call our attention to the alleged health risks associated with drinking milk, at which time it became a topic of conversation at dinner parties, PTA meetings, and health blogs everywhere.

Words are the origin of powerful pieces of information. They represent meaning deeper than the words themselves. So when the conversation about milk began to focus on the health risks, and deliver "proof" that milk is bad, people had to make a choice: accept the words as "truth" and believe the message they were conveying, or dismiss them as "lies" and ignore them altogether.

It's doubtful that one single news article or conversation was enough to get you to pay attention. But, if after a while, the repeated messages started to trigger thoughts like, *"I want to be healthy," "I can't give this to my kids, and risk their health,"* or *"I love ice cream, but it's just not worth it,"* and these thoughts induced feelings of fear, guilt, or internal struggle, that's evidence that your beliefs about milk were being challenged.

And it's likely that once you started to pay attention, you found more and more media messages that further confirmed your new emerging belief: Milk is unhealthy.

If your fridge is now stocked with almond milk (or some other non-dairy variety), your brain chose to accept the messages as truth, and as a result, your belief has changed. However, if the claims about milk did not resonate with you, and instead you thought, *"Those people are crazy! I've been drinking milk my whole life, and I'm just fine,"* then you dismissed the words you heard as lies, and now, anytime the topic comes up, it goes in one ear and out the other, having no effect on you whatsoever. You will continue to go about your life, as always, enjoying milk anytime you want.

Whether we're talking about milk, or any debatable topic, words (and the meaning you give them) are the tipping point to a chain reaction of thoughts, feelings, and ultimately beliefs. But it's not just the words that you hear or read that contribute to your belief system and quality of life. It's also the words you say. Let me demonstrate what I mean.

In Michigan, where I'm from, the weather changes so quickly and drastically that everyone is constantly talking about it.

In the fall though, the small talk tends to take on an entirely different meaning. *"How about this weather?"* becomes a nod to the impending winter. And there are two typical (and opposite) reactions to the realization that winter is quickly approaching.

The first group of people, we'll call them the winter haters, will typically respond with something along the lines of, *"I hate the cold. The days are getting so short; it's so depressing. Summer went by way too fast, as usual!"* For this group, the words *"How about this weather?"* trigger negativity. By giving this phrase a negative meaning, it triggers negative thoughts like shoveling snow, bundling up in layers and layers of clothing, lack of sunshine, being cooped up in the house, drab leafless trees. Obviously, this will lead to pretty nasty feelings like disappointment, dread, misery, and lack of control. So often I hear these people say, *"I don't understand why we live here. Why don't we all just move to Florida?"* And yet, they never do! (Remember those **Energy Vampires** we talked about in chapter 4?) Instead, they continue to complain year after year, play the victim, and choose to be miserable.

Then there's the other group of people who choose to see the silver lining of a Michigan winter. These are the people who filter their reality with positive words. They'll respond to *"How about this weather?"* with: *"I know, it feels amazing! The colors are so beautiful. I love going outside and smelling autumn in the air. It reminds me of camping and cider mills and Halloween. And soon Christmas will be here. My favorite holiday! I hope it snows on Christmas this year! There's nothing more majestic that looking out your window on Christmas morning and seeing the sparkling beauty of freshly fallen snow."*

Such a huge difference, right? This kind of response creates feelings of joy, connection, nostalgia, gratitude, and excitement.

One person suffers in misery all winter long, while the other person embraces the magic and beauty of the seasons. And all because of the words they choose to describe their reality. That's the first major step in changing your beliefs from limiting to empowering: choose your words wisely. Be mindful of using words and phrases that support your desired beliefs and feelings.

So instead of saying, *"I don't have enough money to buy that,"* you might instead ask yourself, *"How can I earn the money to buy that?"* Or instead of, *"Dating is hard. All the good ones are taken. I'll never get married,"* try *"After all this dating experience, I am getting so good at figuring out exactly what I'm looking for, that when I do meet Mr. or Mrs. Right, I'll know right away. It's just a matter of time now."*

Can you feel the difference in those statements? A simple choice of words can mean the difference between feeling disempowered and hopeless to feeling optimistic and completely in control of your life.

Remember, words affect thoughts, which affect feelings which affect beliefs. And in order to effectively transform those core beliefs, you have to start at the surface and work your way through the layers. Words are the surface.

**Words have power.** And we're not just talking about milk or weather. Words have power over every single thought we think and emotion we feel.

Even though most of us were brought up on "Sticks and stones can break my bones, but words can never hurt me," we all know that's a load of B.S. Words of praise, appreciation and acceptance or words of disapproval, judgment or anger can have a powerful impact. For example, think back:

- What's the best compliment you ever received?
- What's the worst thing anyone has ever said to or about you?

Chances are, you remember both of those moments vividly, even though neither happened yesterday. They happened years ago. And yet, the memory of those words (and the way those words made you feel) is as fresh in your mind as if they were spoken only yesterday.

Because we attach meaning to words, those words trigger thoughts that create feelings. And therefore, words matter to us. A lot.

Likewise, the words that we speak to ourselves, about ourselves and the world around us are incessantly impacting us. We may not notice it right away, but those words wriggle their way into our subconscious, take up residence there and then completely alter the way we see things.

Think about some of the things you probably say or hear regularly.

*We can't afford it.*

*I'm broke.*

*This isn't going to work.*

*What's this world coming to?*

*I can't do that. I don't know how.*

*Life is hard!*

*I'd love to, but I don't have time.*

Do these sound familiar? Even if you don't say them, I'm sure you hear them from people around you.

So what's the big deal? Well, there's always more to these words than what may appear on the surface. These statements are all fear-based and often self-defeating. Here's the kicker: If you say something enough times, your brain starts to believe that it's the whole truth and the only truth.

For example, when you continually use the words *"I can't afford it,"* or *"I'm broke,"* your brain recognizes this as a pattern, and it starts to become an automatic response to everything connected to spending money. And no matter how much money you might accumulate, you will continue to feel perpetually broke.

The same thing happens when you say *"I never have enough time,"* or regularly talk about how incredibly busy your life is. No matter how productive and efficient you become, it will always feel like there's more to do than there are hours in the day.

Both of these examples tell your brain and the universe (and everyone around you) that "not enough" is a core definition of your life.

Now that we've discussed the way we are affected by the words we say out loud, let's discuss the words we say to ourselves. Our self-talk. What was the last thing you said to yourself?

Was it, *"You are so beautiful/talented/amazing/sexy"*?

I sure hope so, but I have enough experience to know that it probably wasn't. You probably said something to yourself that you would never in a million years say out loud to your best friend, your daughter or any another human being for that matter.

Think about it. Would you ever look someone you love in the eye and say:

- You look horrible in that outfit. You need to lose weight. A lot of weight!
- You could never make enough money to run a business full-time.
- Why bother, you know you're gonna fail. You've always been a failure.
- You're never going to meet a great partner. You have way too many issues.

Heck no, you wouldn't. Yet, you say things like this to yourself all the time.

When you're not flat out talking smack to yourself, you're

poking fun at yourself and using self-deprecating jokes, on the premise that if you call attention to your flaws first, you're taking away the opportunity for anyone else to judge you or make fun of you. But that assumes anyone else is even thinking that about you in the first place.

- Sure, I'll cook Thanksgiving dinner, as long as you're okay with food poisoning!
- We all know finances just aren't my thing!
- My singing voice is so bad; if I attempted karaoke, there might be a stampede of people trying to rush the exit.
- Trust me! Nobody wants to see me in a swimsuit!

Think of some things you say about yourself. What jokes do you make about yourself? Allow these words to circle around in your head for a second. What thoughts follow these statements? How do they make you feel?

Repeat after me: **The words I say to myself and about myself matter because I matter.**

Are you on board with the idea that words play a crucial role in how the rest of our life goes? Good.

Now, for the sake of creating your new amazing abundant life, you absolutely must start paying attention to the words that come out of your mouth!

Even though words are the easiest layer to take notice of, it's still a new exercise for your mindset muscle. In my experience, the easiest way to train your mindset muscle is with tools and games.

One of my favorite games for becoming aware of the words you use on a regular basis is the *Buzz Word Game.* You may want to recruit some help for this game. Kids are really great at this. They love to call their parents out on stuff. And because I have kids, and I wanted to get them involved in changing their limiting vocabulary too, we invented the *Buzz Word Game*, where we brainstormed all of the negative or "buzz" words and phrases we could think of ("I can't," "I'll never," "I don't know how," and "I should") and wrote them on a list. We then put the list on the refrigerator along with every family member's name. Then, anytime someone got caught using a buzz word they had to put a quarter in a jar and a check mark next to their name. At the end of the week, the person with the least amount of check marks got to keep the quarters. In a house full of kids, this game is super effective! They'll have you transforming your vocabulary in no time.

## Some examples of buzz words and phrases to add to your list are:

### I Can't

Using the words can't or don't imply that you lack the skills, knowledge, power or resources to choose, learn, expand and grow. Sure, there are a few things that might be physically impossible (you physically can't breathe underwater or lift a semi-truck off the ground), but most of the time you use these words because you're giving up on yourself. You're pretending that the choice isn't yours and perhaps even making excuses to prove it. What you're really doing is giving away your power.

> *I can't figure it out.*
> *I can't apply for that job; I don't have the credentials.*
> *I can't sing.*

*I can't start my own business.*
*I can't lose weight.*
*I don't know how*
*I don't have time*
*I don't have money*

### I/ I'll Never:

Never is an absolute. It takes the control away from you and limits what's possible. Using this word keeps you from opening yourself up to new possibilities and trying new things.

*I've never had any luck with dating.*
*I'll never live in my dream house.*
*I'll never make that kind of money.*
*I never travel.*
*I never go dancing.*
*I never wear hats.*

### I Should:

Using this word can have a negative effect on our mindset when it makes us think that we're not doing enough and causes us to feel inadequate.

*I should spend more time marketing on Facebook.*
*I should volunteer more of my time.*
*I should exercise more.*

### Not Enough:

Using this word often suggests that you're afraid of running out. It's a word rooted in scarcity and fear.

*I didn't get enough sleep.*

*I don't have enough.*

*I don't have enough money.*

*There won't be enough food.*

*What if I don't get enough people to buy my offer?*

*Will I impact enough people?*

*Am I enough?*

*Am I doing enough?*

What would happen if you flipped the switch in this disempowering lingo? If you replaced these negative phrases with empowering ones, instead? Read the phrases below and let them process for a few minutes. What images and thoughts do these phrases conjure up? How do they make you feel?

Instead of **I can't**, try:

*I am resourceful. I can figure this out.*

*I can apply for that job! I have mad skills.*

*I might not be Beyoncé, but I can sing a little.*

*I can start my own business. I believe in myself.*

*If I really put my mind to it, I can lose weight.*

Instead of **I/ I'll never**, try:

*I've had a few good dates. And I know I will find "the one" soon!*

*I will live in my dream house!*

*I will make a lot of money. It's coming!*

*I will travel more this year. I'll start by planning a trip to . . .*

*I will make a commitment to go dancing more.*

*I will try on hats next time I'm at the store. I know I'll find one I love!*

Instead of **I should**, try:

*I don't need to spend more time marketing on Facebook. I am energetically aligned with my dream clients, and they are on their way to me in miraculous ways.*

*If I feel called to volunteer more of my time, I will. But I don't feel obligated or pressured.*

*I love my body the way it is. I also love playing. When I feel inspired to play, I will. And I'll get a little cardio in as a bonus!*

Instead of **not enough**, try:

*I am energized and excited to live today to the fullest.*

*I always have enough. I always have more than I need. The Universe always has my back.*

*I have more than enough money. There is always an abundance of money. It flows to me easily and effortlessly. There will be plenty of food.*

*I am attracting people to me that are excited and eager to buy my offer.*

*I make a difference in the lives of others every day just by being myself. I don't need to change the world. I just have to change one person's day. Today, that is more than enough!*

*I am enough!*

*I am doing enough!*

Or, play this game with other adults in your life by making a daily wager—like a cup of coffee, a foot rub or who will cook dinner— to keep it fresh every day. Involving the people in your life that will lovingly call you out, is a creative and effective way to help you recognize (and discontinue) words that disempower and limit you.

If you don't have someone in your life that can help you do that, you can start by noticing other people's word choices. When you're on the phone, at work meetings, family gatherings, or at the mall, listen to what other people are saying. Once you choose to pay attention, you'll become acutely aware of other people's words. Listen and tally up the negativity. Try it for a just a week; it's eye-opening!

Then start analyzing their lives. Don't worry about being judgy; it's just analysis. The people who use an excessive amount of negative words tend to be overwhelmingly dissatisfied with everything in their life—their spouse, their kids, their job, their house. They're miserable. Because what you talk about incessantly becomes your reality.

You probably won't even have to do this for a whole week before you become painfully aware of the truth: That our words determine how we filter the world. And that there is a direct correlation between the words you use and the level of happiness you feel in your life. This truth, though, is a great motivator for change, especially if you discover that what you talk about most is the *opposite* of what you want in your life.

The reality is, that if you're talking about it, you're focusing on it. And, according to the Law of Attraction, whatever you focus on, you're going to get more of.

Why are you spending so much time, energy, and literal air complaining about the things you don't want in your life when you could be talking about (and focusing on) the things you do want?

If you need a solid place to start in changing the negativity in your language, be sure to cut the words Can't, Never, and If out of your vocabulary starting today.

"I **can't** (do/afford/manage/figure out) _____."

"_____ is never going to (work/change/get better)."

"If I ever (find a partner/start a business/lose weight/ win the lotto/) then maybe I'll be (happy/less stressed/ able to relax)."

You probably don't notice how often you're using this kind of limiting language. You'll be surprised once you start paying attention! I mean, something as simple as "I can't open this pickle jar!" can have a negative impact on your core beliefs about yourself and all the things you believe you can't do.

I mean, really? It's a jar. Find another way. You can conquer the jar. I believe in you.

## What to use instead

It's super important to have replacement words because if we don't then we'll just replace the negative words with . . . um . . . silence? That's not helpful. I guess it's a little better than defeating words, but not much.

You need a pocketful of positive words and phrases to use instead that will help you turn your nasty word habits around. For instance:

- "I can't" can be replaced with "I need help with" or "I'm having trouble with"
- "I don't have time" can be replaced with "I'm choosing not to spend time on that"
- "I can't afford it" can be replaced with "That is not a priority for me right now"
- "If I ever find someone" can be replaced with "When I find my soulmate"

Do you see what a difference those slight changes can make? They open up room for possibility and opportunities. They indicate a level of confidence and belief in yourself and your resourcefulness. They suggest that you are in control of your choices and your life. They evoke feelings of empowerment rather than defeat. These tweaks are small, but mighty, in that they put they put you back in the driver's seat. That's what's great about the power of words. Because you are in control, you get to choose whether they bring you down or build you up. It's all about how you choose to use and receive them.

Repeat after me: **I am in control. I believe that what I want is possible. I'm ready to take action!**

How amazing does that feel? Wait, did you say it out loud for real? Seriously, you need to hear the words. Go back and say it out loud.

There you go. Now you feel it!

Now, you may have heard a lot of talk about affirmations. You know, those sayings and proclamations that are supposed to change your life just by repeating them? If it were really that easy, don't you think a lot of the world's problems would cease to exist? The reason affirmations aren't the be-all-end-all miracle solution for transforming limiting beliefs is because it takes a little more than repeating some positive words to create lasting positive change.

While effective, affirmations are only one piece of a complex puzzle with many moving parts. (Yes, in my world, puzzles have moving parts. Just go with it.) I'm not saying affirmations aren't helpful. Actually, I use them myself and recommend them to my clients as an important part of their mindset practice. But because I'm a big fan of compounding the effectiveness of every tool you incorporate into your mindset practice, instead of using regular old affirmations,

I prefer to use **Braffirmations**—affirmations with a little support built in (like a bra).

A lot of people don't like the idea of affirmations or don't resonate with them because it feels like they're just lying to themselves.

*"Money flows easily to me"* feels like a load of B.S. when you can't scrounge up the money to pay the minimum balance on your credit card bill.

*"I am manifesting my soulmate"* feels totally bogus when you're sitting home on a Saturday night, eating Ben and Jerry's straight out of the carton and watching the Notebook, alone.

*"I attract premium clients every day"* feels a little disingenuous when your inbox is empty and so is your bank account.

So, my advice is to create a Braffirmation instead! Here's a formula to follow:

## Supporting words + affirmation + evidence you know to be true

Some ideas for supporting words are:

- *I'm worthy of . . .*
- *I'm capable of . . .*
- *I believe it to be true that . . .*

As for evidence or support, you can either use examples from your own life and experience, or information that shows it's true in someone else's life (remember earlier, when we talked about how our brain likes proof?). Either way, the purpose of a braffirmation is to force your brain to search through its memories to find evidence that effectively supports the affirmative statement.

Here are some real-life examples of Braffirmations from some of my past clients:

"I believe it to be true that I am a colleague of successful entrepreneurs because I have worked alongside several influencers in my industry." —Tara Bosler

When Tara speaks this braffirmation, her brain will immediately set to work looking for evidence that this is true. As her brain searches memories, it finds that, yes, just this month Tara worked with Dana, Jenn, and Stacy, all influencers in her industry. This then, confirms her affirmation and boosts her confidence in herself and her work.

"I believe that everything is falling into place as it should. I know this to be true because I feel it in my gut and I see miracles everywhere." —Stacy Firth

When Stacy speaks her braffirmation, her brain immediately goes to work searching for occurrences that she would label as a "miracles" to prove that everything is, indeed, falling into place. Her brain recalls a recent impromptu podcast interview that resulted in several new clients, and an invitation to speak at an upcoming event. Both occurrences are in alignment with her goals and give her that gut feeling that everything is working out.

"I have the power to transform fear into curiosity and excitement because more and more I'm saying YES to things that initially feel scary." —Julie Neale

For Julie, her brain would go to work looking for recent situations that pushed her outside of her comfort zone. Recalling these memories, and how she conquered her fear, leaves her feeling empowered, confident and ready to tackle anything that comes her way.

"I am a kickass speaker, and I know this because I am constantly being asked to speak and my abilities are being reaffirmed by people I don't even know, reaching out to me to tell me how much they learned and grew from my talks."
—Sharissa Bradley

Sharissa, when speaking her braffirmation, will automatically begin to recall compliments she's received from people who have benefited from hearing her speak. This will help Sharissa overcome her doubt, push through her fears and continue to share her message.

"I am awesome, and I will get this sale! I know this it true because my clients always feel comfortable with me. When my job is finished, they tell me that they really liked working with me and end our visit with a big hug." —Judy Mannino

Sometimes Judy gets in her own head and doubts her abilities to get enough sales to sustain her business. She's fears that her ideal clients will choose to work with a cheaper company instead of her. Saying this braffirmation helps her to reconnect to her value and remember why her clients love her and continue to hire and recommend her. Remembering the hugs and compliments helps her to get out of her head and gives her the confidence to show up as her best self when she's working with clients.

Now, take a minute and create your own powerful braffirmation! Remember to use the formula above. (If you need inspiration or help, come over to our Facebook group for support. We'd love to help you with this! www.tonyarineer.com/facebook.)

Changing your own words is crucial to switching your mindset. Equally helpful is surrounding yourself with people who make similar choices and choose their words carefully, too. Once you start listening and paying attention to the kinds of language and words the people around you use, it will benefit you tremendously to spend more time with the people in your life who use more positive lingo.

Now, don't start whining about how impossible this is because all of your friends, family, and coworkers are a bunch of Negative Nellies. Remember, you have a choice. Go find positive peeps to fill out your inner circle. I promise, they're everywhere! Attend personal development conferences and mindset retreats, go to Meetup events, try out different networking groups. We have the Internet now. Use it!

Since I have chosen to spend more time with positive people, I've started to notice that when you share your dreams, goals, and aspirations with others, it typically goes one of two ways: Negative people will tell you tell you everything they can to prevent you from failing. Positive people, on the other hand, will do everything they can to help you succeed.

It's the difference between someone reacting to your new idea like Eeyore or like Oprah. Which one would you rather hang around with?

I'm going to go ahead and choose Oprah.

Now, if words were all you needed to change to create your Dream Life, everyone would be living chanting their braffirmations every day while living like celebrities. Changing your lingo is only the first step. It's an important step, but it's only the first one.

Next, we will explore one layer deeper: thoughts. Oh, those buggers that can keep you up at night, right? Let's dig into why they have the power to keep defeat you and how you can make your thoughts work for you instead of against you.

# Chapter 7
## Thoughts Layer

Words are easy to detect, right? Because you hear them. Whether they're coming out of your mouth, the mouths of the people around you, or you're saying them to yourself. But thoughts? How do you detect those? They're tricky little buggers, for sure. They can flit in and out of your head, and you may not even notice them until they've already had an effect on you. They don't reside on the surface, and they aren't as obvious as words (or self-talk) and they always take a little more digging to discover. That's why they're a layer deeper than words.

We don't always share our thoughts with others. But just because we don't speak them out loud doesn't mean they don't influence us. In fact, in many cases, that's the very reason why they influence us more. What we think about gets magnified in our heads. How often have you obsessed over something to the point that you got worked up or freaked out?

Have you ever tried calling someone and when they didn't answer, started to worry? Thoughts whirling in your head about how they might have gotten in a car accident. Maybe they're lying in a ditch somewhere. Maybe their blood attracted vampires, and now they're being used as a sacrifice for the dark ones.

Or maybe you've experienced one of those pimple catastrophes. The ones where you tried everything you could to cover it up, but the thing insisted on protruding off of your face like Mount Everest. What you really wanted to do was stay at home and hide from the world until it was gone. But, you promised a friend you'd go out, and the loyal one you are, you braved it in public anyway. You did your best to hide in the corner and avoid conversation, but people insisted on coming up and talking to you. *"Do they have to get right in my face to talk to me?"* Feeling about two inches tall, you were so self-conscious that you couldn't concentrate on anything they were saying. *"Are they looking at me or the alien growing on my face?"* And so the entire evening was humiliating and miserable.

Except, guess what? No one ever noticed the pimple.

In reality, your friend was not abducted by vampires; she just forgot to charge her phone. That was just you letting your thoughts get the best of you. And the pimple was barely even noticeable. But you didn't notice everyone *not* noticing. You created this story in your head about how everyone was staring at your pizza face and then laughing at you for the rest of the night.

Thoughts dictate feelings more than anything else. Thoughts are the reason that you feel the way you do at any given moment. Emotions feel spontaneous, but they actually derive from your thoughts. (Remember back in Chapter 3 when we talked about the chemical response in our brains?)

The connection that I want to dig into here is this: the way we think about ourselves ultimately determines our self-worth. And our self-worth determines how resistant or open to possibilities we are. And that resistance, or openness, determines our reality.

Are the thoughts you have about yourself a direct link to positive self-worth, or not so much?

Do all of our thoughts lead to feelings? No. Sometimes we really do have surface-level thoughts. Like when you go shopping for new jeans. You might try on a pair and think, *"No way! These make me look like an Oompa Loompa!"* Ok, but what does that mean for you? If it means nothing and you just move on to the next pair, it's a surface level thought. But if that thought penetrates deeper and triggers even more self-defeating thoughts *"I'm fat. I'm not attractive anymore,"* and that evokes feelings of ugliness and unworthiness, then it's a self-defeating thought.

It's those self-defeating thoughts that we need to monitor and potentially change.

## Comparison Thoughts

So often we see ourselves the way we *think* others see us. We assume that they're judging and critiquing every decision we make. What's really happening is that we're worried that they're noticing all of the things that we feel insecure about. We're afraid that they'll see our flaws and agree that we're as inadequate as we feel. Our lives then become a constant battle to live up to the imagined expectations of the world. Just thinking about that is exhausting and debilitating. We seriously need to stop doing this to ourselves!

We need to stop comparing ourselves to others. When we do, we're not even comparing apples to apples. Instead, we compare our faults to the perceived strengths of others. We assume that everyone else is living the life they show on Instagram. Let me ask you an honest question. Does your life look like Instagram? I know mine doesn't! Nobody posts pictures of themselves in their maternity sweats (seven years after having the baby) while eating the entire box of Oreos. But tell me that hasn't been your life at some point. It's just that we don't feel comfortable sharing those parts of our lives because they aren't brag-worthy.

We compare our relationship to the relationships of others, thinking theirs is perfect, so we must be doing something wrong. Is anyone's relationship perfect?

We compare our bodies to the celebrities and models we see on the covers of magazines. Maybe God gave them a flawless physique. Maybe it's Photoshop. Or maybe they work really, really hard and have the willpower to say no to pizza and wine. Is that really worth the sacrifice?

We compare our success to the successes of competitors in our industry. They talk about their revenue and how wonderful their business is doing. But what they don't talk about is how much they spent in Facebook ads, affiliate fees, and salaries to make that outrageous income. Or how much time it took. Or how they sacrificed quality family time and their health to get to where they are.

The lives people post on social media and portray to the world makes it look like they have it all figured out, as if they have mastered the secret to effortless success. And when we compare ourselves to that imagined perfection, we're pretty much begging to feel "less than." But we do that to ourselves. I mean, is anyone really looking at us and thinking, *"Gee, she doesn't seem to be keeping up. She's really failing at this whole 'Perfect Life' thing!?"* No! Nobody ever does that! Yet, in our minds, we seem to think that they do.

## Assumption Thoughts

We spend so much time worrying about what other people are thinking, that we end up feeling like nothing we do is enough. We get stuck in that high school mentality of assuming everyone is looking at us and judging us even though the grown-up part of us knows that everyone is way too busy thinking about themselves to be worried about what we're doing or how we look today. And yet, we can't seem to shake that nagging assumption that everyone is watching us, criticizing us, sizing up our flaws and keeping track of our mistakes. Why do we assume that people are thinking these things about us? In a nutshell, because we are thinking these things about ourselves.

> *I'm not pretty enough because I don't look like a Victoria's Secret model.*
> *I'm not smart enough because I know someone that's smarter.*
> *I'm not desirable enough because every ex has cheated on me.*
> *I'm not lovable enough because my dad left when I was little.*
> *I'm not significant enough because I people ignore me when I talk.*
> *I'm not successful enough because someone else makes more money than me.*

## "What If" Thoughts

The "what-if" thoughts come up almost daily for most people. These thoughts are not always so obvious though. The same kinds of thoughts show up when you get a surge of empowerment. You get the courage to rise above those beliefs, but then you're dragged down again by all the "what if's."

It's like when you see a hot guy at the bar, and you're not exactly feeling like a supermodel. I mean, you're wearing your grandma underwear, and you forgot to shave your legs this morning. But you get up the courage (or take a couple of shots of tequila) and start walking over to talk to him. Then as you're walking over, your negative thoughts start flooding in.

*What if he doesn't think I'm pretty?*

*What if he's married?*

*What if he's super smart and thinks I'm dumb?*

*What if I trip?*

*What if things go well and then he notices my hairy legs?*

*What if I say something stupid?*

*What if I spill my drink on him?*

*What if he rejects me?*

And then, you panic. Just as you get close enough to make eye contact, you take a quick turn and head to the bathroom instead because all your "what if" thoughts sucked the confidence right out of you. (And I bet he saw you and thought you were a freakin' knockout and is now totally bummed that you didn't walk over.)

## Fear-Based Thoughts

The same thing happens when you get a big idea or set a big goal. Initially, you get a surge of excitement, but then your negative thoughts move in.

*It's a great idea, but it's going to be really hard to make it work.*

*I'll have to sacrifice a lot.*

*I'll have to talk to a bunch of people. I'm not good at that sort of thing.*

*I should probably get more education or experience, first.*

*It's gonna take a long time.*

*What if it doesn't work?*

*What will people say about me?*

I see this a lot with the entrepreneurs I work with. They will come up with an incredible idea, and then all they think about are the limitations rather than the possibilities, and they end up focusing on the risks rather than the rewards. That is, until we work through this process and they learn how to flip the switch and kick those nasty thoughts to the curb!

Have you ever been there? You want something really, really bad. You set your sights on it, but the end goal seems way too far away. Instead of focusing on the next best step that will move you forward, you focus on all the unknowns and worry about how you will accomplish it and how far outside of your comfort zone those steps will take you. It doesn't take long until you effectively talk yourself right out of going for it. You never even give yourself a chance.

Why do we do this to ourselves?

The reason we fear the unknown and talk ourselves out of doing anything "risky" is because our brains are wired to protect us. Really. It's not entirely your fault, so try not to get too mad at yourself. Fear is a defense mechanism put in place to keep you safe.

Anything outside of your zone of familiarity is a "danger zone" as far as your brain is concerned. Anything that makes you uncomfortable is to be avoided at all costs because the amygdala's (the watchdog of your brain) primary job is to protect you from danger. Your brain doesn't know the difference between being chased by a saber-toothed tiger and a giving a speech at a wedding. If both situations make you uncomfortable, your brain hits the panic button and goes into overdrive trying to get you out of the danger zone and back to familiar territory where it's safe. But that's not the end of this story. Because guess what?

By controlling your thoughts, you have control over how your brain reacts.

We are hardwired to look for the danger that exists around us. Labeling a thought or opportunity as "dangerous" is what keeps your brain (and your life) in the tiny little space where everything is safe and predictable. In this case, predictable means repeating the same thoughts and therefore getting the same results. The same results that have created your world as you know it. Your current reality. But I know that you're unsatisfied with that. That's why you're reading this book. Because you're tired of the same results and you want more, and you're ready to make it happen.

If you want to create a new reality for yourself, you're going to have to start getting intentional with your thoughts and teaching your brain some new tricks, because those old limiting thoughts aren't going to get you to where you want to go.

Yes, we are wired to avoid danger in our external environment to keep us safe and out of harm's way. But what about the dangers in our internal environment? The thoughts that we choose to think about ourselves. What's going on inside our minds is often much worse than anything we'll ever encounter outside of ourselves.

External negativity is rampant. There's no doubt about that. Gossip, judgment, complaining, cattiness. It's on the news, social media, the latest reality show, in line at the grocery store. But you also always have the choice to walk away, shut it off or tune it out, and stop allowing it into your world. I'm sure you can agree that this external onslaught of negativity is toxic. And you'd be better served to eliminate, or at least minimize it, right? But what about the negative thoughts that run on repeat inside your head?

The conversation that runs 24/7 in our heads is always the most influential. If you're not careful, that could be seriously toxic!

I mean, would you tolerate a friend following you around talking smack to you all day? No! So you shouldn't let yourself get away with that either!

If you want to shift your world into alignment with positivity, love, and abundance, you absolutely must start paying careful attention to your internal thoughts. And the moment they start to spew nasty insults your way, shut them down immediately! Do not allow them to have a voice inside your head. Kick 'em to the curb and replace them with thoughts that are encouraging, supportive, and empowering, instead.

The easiest way to create lasting change in the way you think about yourself is to change the way you talk about yourself out loud. Yes, this begins with your words. That's why we spent an entire chapter on it. But, for good measure, I'm going to bring it up again here because of the importance words play on influencing our thoughts—especially when those words become a habit.

Changing the way we talk about ourselves can prove challenging sometimes. Especially considering that we live in a culture that accepts complaining and self-ridicule as normal. It's a way to find common ground and relate to one another (that is, if that's the kind of people you spend most of your time with). It's even modeled in movies and television shows, and it's how many of us have seen adult conversations and friendships modeled.

*Omg! My ass is getting so big! It's gross! I hate the way I look naked.*

*Me too! My love handles are out of control.*

*I hear ya! And don't even get me started about these wrinkles!*

*Oh, I know right? How do the celebrities do it?*

*Please. You know they've had "work" done! If I had that kind of money, maybe then I'd look good too.*

In the above example, these two friends are belittling themselves as a way of bonding with each other. While seemingly innocent, these thoughts can create powerful feelings within us—feelings of guilt, shame, and unworthiness. I know you've had conversations like this. Is this how you really think of yourself? How does that make you feel? It's hard to believe that you're enough and that you can be, do, and have anything you desire when you're thinking thoughts like these. Which is precisely the reason we need to stop the negative self-talk! Can you imagine hearing a conversation that sounds like this?

*Look at me! I am so freakin' sexy! I seriously impress myself.*

*I know, me too! I look good. I feel hot. No . . . I feel like I'm on fire!*

*So do I! You know, I've been thinking; I'm smart, funny, good-looking, I'm a badass entrepreneur, and I can cook! I am one hell of a catch!*

To focus on what you love or appreciate about yourself is typically considered arrogant, egotistical, and conceited. Of course, we don't want to be judged or labeled this way. So instead, we succumb to the cultural norm and belittle ourselves in an attempt to be seen as humble and modest, and therefore accepted.

But what if it wasn't that way? What if acknowledging our strengths and building ourselves (and each other) up wasn't arrogant, egotistical or conceited? What if we started to view it this as a sign of confidence, strength, empowerment, and truth? What if we believed that we are exactly where we need to be and that we're always moving in the direction of our dreams? What if we could make this perspective our new "normal"?

What if all your thoughts about yourself were supportive, empowering, loving, accepting, honest and encouraging? How would this impact your life? How would this affect your decisions? How would it change your beliefs about what you are capable of? How would doing this upgrade what you consider to be "normal" in your life?

The good news is that this can be your new normal! And the even better news is that you don't have to wait. You can start right this second.

All it takes is a choice. Your choice.

My client, Stacy, was running a pattern of negative lingo for far too long. The beginning of her story is something that every single person has experienced. But pay attention to how she noticed her negative thoughts, and switched them up. It can be just this easy!

I had a good life, by most standards. Actually, a great life—an amazing husband, two wonderful children, a beautiful home—but something was off. I wasn't completely happy and couldn't figure out why. I knew something was missing. I knew deep down, that life was not meant to feel like this.

One day as I was meditating, I had what I can only describe as a download of crazy amounts of ideas and information. I'd love to say that the thoughts were mine. But it didn't feel like I came up with them on my own. They were more like ideas flowing through me.

It was in that session of meditating (and then writing it all down) that I came up with an entire plan to run workshops for moms to help them connect to their true purpose and tap into the feelings that they desire most. This idea, this purpose, lit me up like nothing ever had before.

That's when the negative self-talk started:

*"What do you mean you're going to run a workshop? Who are you to teach this? You're still struggling yourself! Who'll want to listen to you? You aren't an expert! No one cares about this stuff anyway. It's just you. Everyone will think you're crazy!"*

I knew that if I was going to do this, I'd have to step away from who I was and the things I've always done and be willing to see myself in a new way. That was scary!

So I started to challenge myself to think differently. Here's the thing, we always doubt our strengths and gifts. We think that because they come easily to us, that they aren't that valuable. That's a lie.

We lie to ourselves all the time. We use words to make up stories in our heads. Those words are rooted in fear and uncertainty. The words whisper, "*You can't do this. You're not good enough. This is going to end really, really badly!*" These words follow you around like haunted shadows, but then you realize that's all they are, just shadows. Scary stories lurking in your imagination that aren't true.

I've flipped the switch on my own scary dialogue by acknowledging it, challenging it, and replacing it with words that fuel me rather than deflate me.

When I go on a tangent of negative self-talk, I first acknowledge it by saying to myself, "*Oh, that's interesting. I just spent that last 2 minutes going to a bad place because something triggered me. What if my daughter thought that about herself? Would I allow that? No! And besides, is that really true? No. No, it's not! I'm just as equipped to teach as anyone else. I may be learning, still, but that makes me relatable. And there are people who need to hear this message. And they want to hear it from me. I am confident in myself and what I offer. I can do this. Not because I have to, but because it feels right. And it doesn't matter what people think. I'll show up, be my best self, make a difference where I can, and I will continue to be proud of myself, love myself and accept myself, no matter what.*"

The truth is that the things in my life that made

me feel like I was failing have always turned out to be a positive experience in the end.

I remind myself of that when those whispers start to creep in. And to drown the negative self-talk out, I turn to my positive affirmations and mantras, which I pair alongside visualization to make them more powerful. I visualize myself inhaling confidence and exhaling all my doubts and allow myself to really feel it.

Did you notice the switch? It happens quickly, but the result is powerful. It only takes an instant to acknowledge negative thoughts and turn them into empowering thoughts instead. A single moment. A single choice. Once you become aware of your self-talk, and how it's affecting your reality, you have the power to make a different choice.

For real, it's time to stop all the negative talk. Seriously. Stop it right now! It's up to you. Start noticing it, calling it out, and changing it. It will make a world of difference.

I know what you're thinking: *"Oh sure, just start noticing my self-talk. How am I supposed to do that?!"* I know, easier said than done, right? Our thoughts, especially the self-defeating ones, have been running through our minds for so long that we barely notice they're there. They're like evil little subliminal whispers that operate in the dark shadows just outside of our awareness. That's why we have to hunt them down and bring them out of the shadows and into the spotlight.

The easiest way to start noticing your negative, self-defeating thoughts is to get purposely aware of what you're saying about yourself. How you're secretly and silently describing yourself. How you talk to yourself.

Start by making a list of everything you *think* is wrong with you. What?!? I'm serious! Go ahead and write down all the stuff that you don't like and then maybe add a couple of things that you continue to tolerate about yourself but feel are less than perfect. (Feel free to turn to the Discover section of the workbook and complete the Mirror Work exercise if you want to go deeper with this right away.)

And then, take a look at that list and count out everything you wrote down. Then, for every item on that list, write down three things that you love about yourself. These can be strengths, skills, characteristics, whatever comes to mind. The only rule is that you have to believe that they are true.

Was that difficult? Perhaps a little uncomfortable? Good! Discomfort is normal, and it's a sign of progress.

Now, since we're on a roll, let's get a little more uncomfortable in the name of progress. Take your list of things that you love about yourself and go stand in front of a mirror. Yes, I'm serious! Now, look yourself in the eye and say some of those lovely and amazing things to yourself out loud.

> *I am beautiful, inside and out.*
> *I am hilarious/kind/generous/smart, etc.*
> *I am a kickass writer/dancer/cook/marketing strategist.*
> *(Whatever it is that you are freakin' amazing at!)*

Make it a habit of giving yourself three genuine compliments, like this, every day. Stand in front of the mirror, look directly into your eyes and tell yourself three things that make you feel confident, strong, empowered, and special. Set a reminder on your phone, put post-it notes up to remind you, or agree to do this with a friend—whatever it takes to start making this a daily routine!

This practice will disrupt your current brain pattern and will help you to create a new, positive pattern.

You have to intentionally and consciously disrupt the pattern; you can't just decide you're going to choose a new pattern and assume your brain will be on board—because I can almost guarantee that it won't be. Your brain will fight to go back to the familiar groove that it's used to every single time. (Remember the Brain Truck?) Be patient and remind yourself that the old groove isn't serving you anymore and that you have this new one now where you say nice things to yourself.

It might go like this for a while:

You see someone who is good-looking and in great shape.

> Brain: "*Ugh, I'm never going to have a body like that.*"
> You: "*Oooh, I recognize that thought. I know we've been saying that one for a long time, but we aren't doing it that way anymore. Now we are thinking: I'm attractive and amazing!*"
> Brain: "*Hmm . . . I don't know if I can get behind that. I'll never look like that.*"
> You: "*I'm attractive and amazing, remember?*"
> Brain: "*Oh yeah! Okay!*"

Your brain might fight with you for a little while, but remember: You are in control. And you have the power to get into a new groove and create a new thought pattern. Even if it takes a while to get a handle on it, you will do it. And then one day you'll realize you haven't compared yourself to anyone in a while because you were too busy thinking positively about yourself!

You just have to become aware of the thought first, and then choose something different.

Remember that with time and practice, it will no longer require a conscious effort. It will become a habit and your new normal. How amazing will it feel to have default thoughts that lift you up and empower you rather than rip you to shreds? It is possible, and it's easier than you might think. I believe in you. You can do this!

A client of mine, Judy, is an excellent example of how this shift can happen. She was working a 9-5 and desperately wanted to turn her side hustle into a full-time business, but anytime she thought about leaving the security of her job (and the medical benefits it provided) she'd start to panic. She'd think to herself, "*I don't know if I can quit my job and do this full time. I don't know if I have what it takes to keep money coming in steadily.*"

On mornings when she had a client meeting scheduled, she'd wake up feeling anxious and nervous. She questioned herself and whether or not she'd get the sale.

Until she changed her thoughts.

She started becoming aware of the way she was talking to herself, the words she was using, and the way she was thinking. When the negative self-talk would start, she'd say, "*Wait a minute. Stop that right now!*" Then, she'd walk over to the mirror, look at herself and say "*You CAN do this! You are awesome!*" sometimes repeating herself until the fear simmered down and the confidence took over.

After doing this, Judy remembers: "*I'd feel all geeked and amazing, and then I'd go see my client, and I'd feel confident and ready for anything!"*

The result of this transformation is that she no longer just hoped for the sale, she expected it. And that's exactly what she got! In just a matter of months, Judy was able to leave her full-time job. And now, she makes in a single day what it took her six weeks to make at her 9-5 job! How's that for a transformation?

You can see the power of changing your words and your thoughts. It takes some effort, but it's pretty simple to notice those and begin to create new habits. And here's the kicker: those layers are *essential* to transform before deciding to tackle the Feelings Layer. But you're ready! Let's do it!

The way we think about
ourselves ultimately
determines our
self-worth.
And our self-worth
determines how resistant
or open to
possibilities we are.
And that resistance, or openness,
determines our reality.

# Chapter 8
## Feelings Layer

It's been said that people are more afraid of public speaking than they are of dying! I am not surprised by this because I was once one of those people! When I first started on this journey of becoming a coach, I was beyond terrified of public speaking. But I knew it was a fear I'd have to overcome, so I joined Toastmasters. Toastmasters is a club where you show up every week and either give a speech in front of the other club members, or you listen to other people's speeches and give constructive criticism and feedback so that they can improve. Every time I gave a speech, I brought my husband, Tom, to sit in on the meeting and videotape me from the back of the room so that I could watch myself and refine my delivery.

My first couple speeches were safe. I played small. They were subjects that everyone could agree on, so they didn't freak me out. It wasn't until I showed up for my third speech that the panic kicked in. This subject I chose to talk about was closer to my heart. It was a vulnerable and controversial speech about mindset, self-worth, and the effect it had on women (myself included).

There was a woman in the group that was an Empowerment Coach. I respected, and kind of idolized her because she was already doing what I wanted to be doing. She knew all kinds of big-name people and had fancy credentials. I was constantly comparing myself to her. *"She's so poised. She seems so confident. She's already making a great living doing this. She's so successful. Will I ever be as good as her?"*

The day I was set to deliver my (scary as hell) speech, I wondered if she would be in the room that night. Sure enough, when I walked into the room and saw her, any shred of confidence that I was scrambling to hang onto disappeared. I thought, *"I know I'm here for critique, but what if she calls me out and tells me I'm wrong?"* I made up this story in my head that ended in her judging me. In my mind, I painted her as the biggest critic ever to walk the earth.

My thoughts surrounding this woman's judgment (which I totally made up) triggered feelings of anxiety, and then panic, and finally, shame. I thought, *"Who do you think you are to stand up and share this message? You want to be this person that lifts up and empowers other women, but you're a hot mess! Look at you. You're struggling with your own self-worth right now. Who are you to give advice on how to be confident? You're not good enough to be here."* I was on a bullet train going full speed ahead into the dismal tunnel of shame.

When it was nearing my turn to speak, I could feel my palms sweating. I could hear my heart pounding in my head. I felt dizzy and weak.

By some miracle, I managed to stand up and walk up to the podium. I took a deep breath and started to speak. I barely got through the introduction when I looked at the woman I idolized and saw that she was staring at me with no expression on her face whatsoever. I needed her to be responding, and she wasn't. I needed her validation, her approval that it was okay for me to be talking about this. Instead, all I got was a blank, expressionless stare. At that moment, any shred of dignity I had, was lost.

I forgot everything. I couldn't remember what I was supposed to be talking about. I couldn't remember what to say next. I honestly couldn't even remember my name. I blanked-out. Shaking almost

The Mindset Switch

uncontrollably, I started fumbling around at my notes, hoping to regain my composure, but my vision was so blurry that I couldn't even read the words I had written down. The president of the club came up to me at the podium, touched my arm and told me to step off the stage and take a break, regroup and try again.

I was humiliated. I felt like a complete failure. And, of course, Tom was recording the whole thing.

I didn't think it was possible to feel completely exposed and yet totally invisible at the same time. I was mortified. All I wanted to do was run for the door, delete all these people from my Facebook and forget it ever happened. Forget my career as a speaker, as a coach, as a leader in a movement to empower other women.

I seriously considered giving up on my dream and going back to my normal and safe world where there was no judgment, comparison or shame.

But I didn't. Because if I didn't redeem myself, I knew I couldn't hide from it. After all, it was recorded. Tom saw the whole thing. I had to make a different choice. A stronger, braver choice.

I ended up stepping into the hallway to regroup and attempt to muster up whatever confidence and control I could. It took me a solid five minutes of building myself up—saying nice things to myself and visualizing myself getting through the whole speech with ease—before I could talk myself into going back in there and trying again. When I did, I nailed it, and it felt great.

But, the panic that manifested into a physical reaction was all made up in my head. It began with the words I used to describe myself that summoned negative thoughts that resulted in disempowering feelings of panic, humiliation, failure, insignificance, and shame.

That's how fast this can happen. In a matter of minutes our words, thoughts, and feelings can manifest into our reality. If we don't choose something different, that reality will continue to exist.

We often think that feelings happen to us. That they're spontaneous and occur as a result of what's going on around us, and there's no way to control or change them. We just have to choose to feel them or, if the feeling is unwanted, repress them, avoid them or ignore them, right?

Actually, no. We *do* have control over our emotions—even before they happen. Sure, we'll still have spontaneous feelings that pop up, but they don't define us. That's not their purpose. Their job is to *clue us into* what we should focus on, not control us or consume us.

Just knowing that offers a tiny piece of liberation. Our emotions don't have to control us (or the way we react to the world)!

Panic doesn't have to get the best of us or make us run and hide. We can gain control of our thoughts, and therefore control our emotional response, which then will create the kind of experience we desire.

If I had chosen to use different words and thoughts to describe myself and this other woman, I would have had a completely different experience during my speech. If I hadn't assumed she was my biggest critic, or that I had no place there, or that I needed her approval to validate me, I know I wouldn't have triggered within myself the panic and shame that I did that night.

After making a new choice—choosing to empower myself with confidence by engaging in positive self-talk and visualizing the outcome I wanted—I was able to change my experience. It went from utter failure to ultimate success.

You might be wondering what happened with that woman. You might be waiting for the moment when she and I connected, and she told me everything she was thinking. But there wasn't a moment like that. I have no idea what she was really thinking. And you know what? I don't care. It doesn't matter to me. What she thought about me and my performance (if anything at all) means nothing to my story and what I bring to the world.

Now, I'm not telling you to ignore your feelings by any means! Because while emotions do not have direct power over us, they are incredibly powerful and useful. Emotions inherently create our reality. The way you feel about something will determine what you choose to surround yourself with, focus on, and allow into your life. Your feelings create your reality.

Your **feelings** determine your **vibration**.

Wait, what in the what does *that* mean?

Basically, our understanding of atoms is more like waves of energy than static matter. Subatomic particles behave in ways that seem incomprehensible to our general understanding of natural laws, and yet, they are constantly in motion, vibrating all around us and even inside of our bodies. (Go ahead and search "quantum physics" or "quantum mechanics" on YouTube and prepare to have your mind blown!)

Waves inevitably move, constantly. That movement is called "frequency" and based on the speed at which it moves, is labeled low or high frequency or "vibration." Everything has a vibration. Yes, objects, but also words, thoughts, feelings, and beliefs! Similar vibrations are attracted to each other. So *high vibrating stuff* is attracted to other high vibrating stuff, and the same is true with low vibrating stuff. So, your feelings determine your general vibration, which is what works to attract other stuff into your life.

Pay attention. Is your vibration high or low? Because that's what determines what you're attracting into your life.

A feeling in and of itself isn't going to change your whole world right this second. As Dr. Joe Dispenzia described in the film *The Science of Changing Your Mind*, the repeated occurrences of a certain feeling will start to influence our view of the world. When a certain **feeling** is maintained long enough, it becomes a **mood**. When you continue to stay in that mood for an extended period of time, it becomes a more permanent part of your personality. The more you display that part of your **personality**, it can attach itself to your **identity**.

This is how we often describe people.

*She's just so miserable all the time.*
*He is selfish and doesn't think about anyone else.*
*She has such a magnetic, positive personality; people just love being around her!*
*He's so funny and upbeat; I'm always laughing when we're together.*

Each of those statements speaks to an identity and personality trait but starts with a feeling. (Unworthy, lacking, positive, joyful, respectively.)

Take a minute to think about how others are likely to describe you. What's your personality like? Is that consistent? Is that *who you are*? Do you want it to be that way? And what about the people you're around all the time? Do you like those personalities and how they make *you* feel?

What you focus on affects the words you use, the thoughts you think, and the emotions you experience—all of which will determine your reality. Each experience you have is going to be filtered through that reality. If your default feeling is resentment, for example, you'll start to only notice (and focus on) the negativity in your life; all of the things that don't work out and make you angry.

One of my clients would tell me about her family, which had a few "Eeyores" in it. I mean, we all like that lovable donkey from Winnie the Pooh, but when we're faced with an Eeyore in real life, it can be frustrating at best and debilitating at worst.

During the early days of my client's business success, she would talk about how well things were going and would encourage others in her family to try entrepreneurship, especially when they would complain about their jobs or talk about how they work all the time.

*"Start a side hustle!"* she would say.

*"Open your own business!"* she would suggest.

And then the onslaught of Eeyore would begin. We've all heard it; the seventeen (thousand) reasons why it wouldn't work, it takes too much time/energy/money/effort, it would fail anyway because everyone is already doing it.

But my client knew the truth: if you decide to make it work, it will! She's focused on the endless possibilities and positive expectations of success. And guess what? It's working!

And the Eeyores? Well, for now, they're still complaining about the jobs they hate.

See the connection? Words, thoughts, and feelings . . . they all contribute to our reality.

Let's take a minute to look at how some of these prolonged feelings play out. Caution: specific people may come up in your mind as you read these examples. Keep track of that because you may want to rethink how much time you spend with them, now that you understand the role your surroundings play in creating your reality.

## Feeling: VICTIMIZED

You assume that the world is against you. You're constantly guarded, skeptical and suspicious. You tend not to trust people and put walls up.

Your Mantra: *"It's not my fault."*

Your words cater to the *"I'll believe it when I see it"* mindset. Other common phrases: *"I doubt that's going to happen,"* *"That sounds too good to be true,"* and *"I'm just unlucky."* Life just "happens" and its happenings usually aren't in your favor. You live your life in reaction mode, feeling that most situations are beyond your control. Your general disposition feels disempowering, and defeat becomes a self-fulfilling prophecy.

## Feeling: UNWORTHY

You see yourself as unworthy and have even referred to yourself as broken. Damaged. Not _____ (fast, young, smart, pretty, experienced, extroverted, up-to-par, etc.) enough to get what you really want. You see the situation for what it is, and you settle for what you can get. Because you don't see yourself as deserving enough, you continue to play safe and small. You stay where you're comfortable, and you know, with relative certainty that you can predict the results. While those may not be the ideal results, at least they're without risk.

Your mantra: *"At least it's better than nothing."*

This mindset shows up in your love life, personal life, and work life. Your innermost thoughts are like a broken record whispering,

*"I'm not good enough,"* and you find that you're constantly comparing yourself to others, to the person you used to be, and to the person you'd like to be. But in your mind, no matter what you do, you just don't measure up.

You have it in your head that you should fit a certain mold. That to be rich, successful, loved, accepted or deemed worthy, you must look and act a certain way. When you don't, you get down on yourself by telling yourself you're not enough. You lose faith in what is possible and end up setting for what is.

## Feeling: GUILT

You just can't seem to get anything right. You obsess over past events. Over the actions you took (or didn't take) and the things you said (or shouldn't have said). No matter what you do, someone always seems to get hurt.

After an event happens, you obsess for hours, playing it over and over in your head. I shouldn't have said this. I should have done that. I shoulda, coulda, woulda and maybe I wouldn't feel like shit right now.

Your mantra: *"Nothing I ever do is right."*

You are a people-pleaser by nature. And more than anything, you want to feel connected, loved, and accepted. But you judge your behavior harshly. You take on the emotions (and often imagined emotions) of the people you love.

This makes it hard to forgive yourself and leaves you feeling like the "bad guy," or like your choices and behaviors let someone you care about down (your spouse, your parents, your children, your friend, your boss, yourself). You allow the memories of these less-than-ideal behavior choices to play out in your mind and convince yourself that you are undeserving of the love and acceptance you crave.

Feelings of guilt have a way of manifesting into invisible blocks that stop you from believing you deserve the help, support, love, and acceptance of others. You fear being a burden and find it difficult to ask for help. When it's offered, you turn it down. On the inside, you need to feel emotionally supported, but on the outside, you simply say, *"No thanks, I'm ok."*

## Feeling: SUPERIORITY

*"Life would be easier and better if everyone else would just change and do things **my** way!"* is your battle cry.

You. Judge. Everything. And you get especially frustrated when someone doesn't measure up to your standards. You criticize the way other people drive. How they discipline (or don't discipline) their children. How clean (or messy) their house is. How they dress. How they communicate. You make judgments about where they live. The car they drive. The music they listen to. You get frustrated over how long it's taking the person in front of you at the grocery store to check out. You want to scream: *"You're doing it wrong! I have a better way!"* (And sometimes you do.)

All of the constant judgment makes you feel like life is hard. Your words become blame-based and rooted in unsolicited advice.

Your mantra: *"People suck."*

Not only do you have high standards for the people around you, but you also have extremely high standards for yourself. You strive for perfection in everything you do. When your work, behavior, or performance is less than perfect, you turn that judgmental finger on yourself. Deep down, you fear that if you're less than perfect, you'll lose the love and acceptance of others. Your greatest fear is that you'll be left behind, phased out, or abandoned.

## Feeling: SHAME

Shame is an emotion that we rarely talk about. But it's one that we all feel deeply at some point, and in some cases, bury deep within ourselves allowing it to sabotage our sense of self-worth.

We all make poor choices and act in ways we're not proud of. But when we allow that feeling of shame to define who we are, it becomes toxic. When we experience shame, our instinct is to try to forget about it as soon as possible. Dealing with the painful emotion would mean having to feel it all over again, and who wants that? So, we ignore it, burying it deep within our subconscious, and we do our best to pretend it never happened.

When you allow yourself to feel ashamed of who you are because of the choices you've made or the things you've done, you hold yourself captive inside a world of limitations. In other words, you stay stuck in the mud! That shame (as well as the resistance to forgiving and releasing it) holds you back by tricking you into thinking that you are a bad person and that that you're unworthy of the things you want. When you hold onto shame, you end up hiding your true self from the rest of the world.

Your mantra: *"If I don't draw too much attention to myself, no one will know what a mess I really am."*

The truth is that you're not a mess at all! Actually, you're perfect. But because you haven't forgiven yourself for some aspect of your past, you're having a hard time believing that. Instead of loving who you've become as a result of those choices, you're hiding behind a façade of who you think you're supposed to be. So you're careful to reveal only the aspects of yourself that you believe the world will see as acceptable. It's a distraction to hide what's going on deep beneath the surface.

You want to protect yourself from further pain, so you stay small and play it safe. You don't want to fail in front of anyone. You don't want people to see the imperfect side of you. You keep your walls up and your audience at a safe, manageable size and distance. As long as you maintain some semblance of control, you'll be able to manage the image you want the world to see.

Do any of these profiles sound familiar?

Do you know people that fit each of these profiles? Do you resonate with one (or more) of these descriptions? Maybe not all the time, but some of the time. We all do at some point or another. To fit one of these profiles is to be human, and, quite frankly, normal!

The problem isn't experiencing this on the rare occasion. It's allowing these profiles to become your default personality. It's allowing yourself to stay in a certain emotional state for so long that it causes your life to play out differently.

Do you want to know a fun little fact that has the potential to change everything you've ever known about emotions?

**An emotional state only lasts for 90 seconds.**

Yes. Literally 90 seconds. Or less. That's it.

If you are experiencing an emotion for longer than that, it's because you keep replaying the thoughts in your head that tell your brain to release the chemicals necessary to keep feeling those feelings.

*"Wait, you mean I'm doing this to myself?!"*

Sorry sweetheart, but yes.

Have you ever been mad at someone? Like so mad you were

on the verge of either choking them or breaking down into a fit of tears? Only, in an effort to break the tension and lighten the mood, the person you were mad at tried to make you laugh? But you weren't ready to laugh. You were still fumingly pissed off, and you didn't want to let them off so easily. So instead of focusing on the funny jokes they keep spewing your way, you remained focused on the situation that pissed you off? In your mind, you had to keep replaying the scenario to stay mad; otherwise, you knew you'd crack and this whole game of "I'm right, and you're wrong" would be over.

That's because we are wired to experience a given emotion for about 90 seconds, but so often we pull ourselves back into it over and over again by continuing to think about it. Sometimes on purpose. Sometimes by pure default of how we've been conditioned to react. Our brain is trying to deal with it, but we overcomplicate the process and end up forcing ourselves to keep reliving emotions that feel awful.

But not you. Now that you're educated on how long emotions last (and how to control them), you no longer have to remain a victim to negative emotions. You now have the power to notice your emotions as they're happening in real time, and if they aren't benefiting you, you can choose to focus on a better thought, which in turn will produce a better emotional response. You get to choose how you're going to feel about anything and everything, simply by choosing how you think about it!

When was the last time you were stood up? I know it's happened to you. You had plans with someone, and you were all excited to go out. You spent hours picking out the perfect outfit, doing your hair and makeup and imagining how the night would turn out. Then, out of the blue, you get a text that says little more than, *"I have to cancel. Sorry.*" And you're crushed. You feel a wave of emotion:

**Devastation**: "*I was so looking forward to this. Now my night is ruined.*"

**Anger:** "*How rude! Nothing like waiting till the last minute to cancel.*"

**Abandonment:** "*Did something better come up?*"

**Insecurity:** "*Am I not good enough?*"

This 90-second wave of emotion lasts exactly that—90 seconds. Then you are faced with the choice to continue to think negatively focused thoughts or think a new thought. You know how it usually goes: you allow your imagination to run wild and paint a picture of your friend out with someone else, having more fun than ever, with complete disregard for your feelings. You end up putting your sweats on, turning on E! TV, and eating ice cream and peanut butter straight out of the jar.

But what if, at that 90-second mark, you focused on better thoughts instead? What if you thought to yourself, "*Well, I'm already all dressed up. And I look pretty freaking good if I do say so myself. I wonder who else I can call to go out with? I know someone must be itching for a night on the town!*"

Focus is everything when it comes to feelings. This rule isn't just applicable to one-time incidents. What you focus on, consistently, becomes your reality.

I know you've seen this happen. Think about the people in your life. Do you know people that grew up in the same house and the same family but are now opposites of each other with completely different viewpoints on life? Of course, you do! We all do!

I know two sisters, Lisa and Beth, who grew up together in the same house and with the same people around them. They had a rough upbringing, complete with booze, drugs, and sexual abuse. Beth wallowed well into adulthood and chose to feel the fear and scarcity of being a continual victim. Lisa, on the other hand, decided those feelings didn't serve her. She chose to be positive. She flipped her switch by choosing to feel generous and appreciative. She chose to live her life looking for the silver lining.

I will give you one guess as to which one is still struggling and which one is happy and successful. You guessed it. Beth is still reliving those same emotions from childhood and doing her best to numb them with drugs. Lisa, on the other hand, is a happily married mother of two kids, and a successful doctor. She has learned to find gratitude and forgiveness in her past because it allows her help others who are suffering. Don't get me wrong, flipping the switch, especially when coming out of challenging circumstances like this is not easy! But it's the only option if you want to take control of your life.

So, what about you? What feeling will you choose to let go of? What feeling will you focus on instead?

Instead of choosing to feel *victimized, unworthy, guilty, superior or ashamed*, what if you chose to focus on *generosity, appreciation, love, and joy*? Well, let's see how those play out:

## Feeling: GENEROSITY

You continually ask, *"How can I serve/give?"* because you know there's more than enough to go around. You know that there's an abundance of resources and your cup will fill up again and again.

You're generous with praise, gratitude, and resources. You look for ways that abundance shows up in your life through time, money, love, and joy so that you can share what you have with those around you.

My beautiful client and friend, Veronica once said to me: "*I believe that there is a cup in heaven that collects your good deeds. When that cup is full, the good deeds overflow and start coming back to you.*" It's a beautiful sentiment to live by.

The thing about being tuned into the vibe of generosity is that you must do it without any expectation of getting anything in return. You know that eye for an eye mentality? Throw it out! It will just taint your good deed, and it won't count toward filling your cup. Your generosity must come from a place of pure desire to help and nothing more.

My husband's best friend, Anthony, was the middle of three children. When he was thirteen, he lost his fifteen-year-old brother, Mark, to a heart condition. Anthony had grown up experiencing Christmas, but after losing his brother, the family decided that instead of doing Christmas the typical way, they wanted to do something different. They wanted the holiday season to be about spending quality time with those you love while you're here on this earth to do it. So, instead of exchanging gifts, they decided to donate to charity in addition to tithing at their church. They instilled in their children their deep sense of generosity and abundance. They never worried, "*Is there going to be enough for us?*" Their focus was on giving and serving others.

When I first met this family, I felt bad for them. I couldn't imagine growing up without the anticipation of giant gift-wrapped toys under the tree. "*What a punishment,*" I thought. "*Those poor kids!*" It wasn't until years later that I realized what this tradition did for them, and realized what a blessing and a gift the tradition really was. The adults they grew up to be are the most generous and abundant-minded people I've ever met. They give selflessly whenever they can and they never even whisper a word of scarcity.

They believe that God will continue to provide and it will always be okay.

Their investment in the well-being of others shows up in everything they do. They show gratitude to every single person around them—friends, family, co-workers, but also strangers, like servers at restaurants. They will make sure to use the server's name several times, ask about their life and show genuine interest in what they have to say. They are always mindful of demonstrating true appreciation for those around them.

The whole family is generous not just through their financial donations, but also through their words, actions, and time. They show up. They literally, physically show up to events to give their support. They go out of their way to let other people know they matter.

Has it paid off? Definitely! Anthony lives an abundant and prosperous life. He's happily married with two beautiful children, is a successful entrepreneur and continues to give and give and give. He is someone I admire and look up to for the simplistic ways in which he views the world: just love one another as yourself and have faith that everything will always be okay.

Your actions of giving, showing up, and being generous are what fill up your Abundance Cup—the cup that keeps on giving! The more you fill it up with your generosity, the more abundance will overflow back into your life.

## Feeling: APPRECIATION

You understand that gratitude is a lifestyle. Appreciation isn't just something you do; it's a way of life.

Your mantra: *"Everything always works out for the best."*

You truly believe that. Your reality is rooted in positivity and abundance. You don't ask questions that begin with "if." Instead, you make statements that are built on "when" and "will." *When I am on the Ellen Show. When I make six-figures. When I buy my dream house with the big windows on the lake. I will meet Mr. Right. I will be a successful business owner. I will take a year off to travel. I will do it because I believe that the Universe is working in my favor.*

And while you're waiting for the Universe to deliver all your abundance, you're grounding yourself in the present moment and feeling strong feelings of gratitude for everything in your life. *I am grateful for my success. I am grateful for money. I appreciate my current home. I am thankful for the men I've dated so far (they've all helped me identify what I don't want so I could get clear about what I do want). I am grateful for the freedom I have.*

And when things don't work out the way you expected them to, you're still grateful. You find the silver lining, and find gratitude in the lesson that the situation was there to teach you. *I am grateful for my mother-in-law who continues to teach me insightful new lessons about boundaries.* With every challenge you overcome, you expand, learn, and grow into a better version of yourself. You know that without those challenges, that growth wouldn't be possible. And for that, you are especially grateful.

Overall, you have a positive outlook and constantly find reasons to be thankful—both big and small.

Wow! How would your life be different if you woke up and lived all your days like *that!?*

## Feeling: JOY

You look for fun, excitement, and playfulness in all that you do. You find ways to make everyday activities enjoyable for you and those around you. Traffic-light dance parties, stand-up comedy at a business conference, sending a silly light-hearted note along with your electric bill. Nothing is mundane or boring when you choose to add an element of fun to it.

You have no shame in your childlike wonder and find joy in the small things and awe in the big things. You're curious about how things will work but don't dwell on outcomes. You find ways to play and celebrate along the journey instead of waiting until you've "accomplished" something. You know that the real celebration can be in everything we do if we are tuned in to what brings us joy.

Your mantra: *"Let's play!"*

When living from a place of joy, you are especially tuned in to living in the moment. When you experience pure joy, there is nothing else distracting you from it. Think about the last time you laughed until you cried. That is joy. That is living in the moment.

## Feeling: LOVE

You approach everything with your heart first. You lead your life and make your decisions from a place of love and compassion. For you, there are no limits. Happiness, success, expansion! Love makes all things possible.

You look for ways that everyone can "win" in every situation. You know that love creates abundance, so there's no need to compete or make decisions based on an assumption of scarcity. Love expands to include everyone and all things, and so do you.

Your mantra: *"All you need is love!"* (And you're more than willing to give that love out!)

You see the good in people no matter what. You know that when they are angry, mean, and miserable, that they are just lost, fearful souls crying out to be loved. And you do your best to let them know they are worthy and deserving of that love. It could be a simple as a wink or a smile, as innocent as a compliment or a hug. You might even send them your loving energy through a thoughtful prayer. You know that love heals everything, and so you do your best to offer it and reconnect people to it whenever you can.

Because you know that you are love, in its purest form, it's easy for you to reconnect with that feeling of total acceptance. You will fall down. You will mess up. You will get frustrated, angry, and sad. But no matter what, you accept yourself for who you are, and you deeply and completely love yourself. Always.

Appreciation, Joy, and Love are the emotions that align you with the highest vibration there is. It is in this vibrational frequency we all strive to align with. It is here where the struggle and worry of everyday life and stress disappears, and all feels right with the world. It is here that you are connected to source energy, the Universe, God.

Anything you desire can be yours. Just get on board and tune in to what you desire to feel. And do your best to connect with these high vibration feelings as much as possible.

Don't wait. Give yourself permission to feel that way now. You have control over that part, too. No more, *"I'd feel abundant if I made x-amount of money,"* *"I'll be happy (and I'll feel love) when I meet the perfect partner,"* *"I'll feel successful when I'm able to buy my dream house,"* *"I'll feel worthy when my parents finally tell me they are proud of me and the choices I've made in my life."*

Don't put conditions on your feelings. You don't have to wait to feel worthy of feeling the way you want to feel. You don't have to earn it. You don't have to get something or accomplish something to feel these things. You don't need the stars to align to feel amazing, and you certainly don't need someone else's permission, approval or validation before you get to start feeling all those warm and fuzzy emotions you desire. Choose to feel them today with what you have already.

Which then, begs the question: How do you want to feel?

Abundant? Happy? Successful? Secure? Sexy? Brilliant? Playful? Connected?

Get super clear about that. Write it down. (Get started on this right now by turning to the *Desire Map Exercise* in the Dream section of the Workbook.)

What's stopping you from feeling that? Go ahead, give me the list of all the things that are standing between you and feeling amazing because they're not legit reasons at all. They're excuses.

# Chapter 9
# Let's Start (and then Stop) with the Excuses

It's acceptable (and normal) to be at a dinner party and complain about how swamped you are with work, how overly busy your life is, or why everyone else is the problem in your world, right? You haven't met the love of your life because all the good ones are taken. You haven't started your business or leveled up because your kids are consuming all your time, or because your spouse is unsupportive or because Mercury retrograde keeps getting in the way. You haven't scheduled that vacation because money is tight, the kids are in sports, the stars haven't aligned yet. It has nothing to do with you, at all. That's the kind of "reality" that's socially accepted and normal to talk about.

What if instead, you came to terms with what you're really feeling? If you did, you'd probably say something along the lines of, *"I'm feeling a little vulnerable. I'd really like to do this thing, but I'm afraid people aren't going to love me the same way."* Or, *"I'm afraid of exposing myself and risking people seeing me for who I really am."* Or, *"I so badly want to take this risk, but I'm afraid of what I'll have to give up or what I might lose if I do."* Or, *"Deep down I'm*

*afraid if I do meet 'the one,' I'm going to fall hardcore, and he (or she)
is going to see all my flaws and won't feel the same way about me,
and I'll end up hurt.*"

Yikes! That's uncomfortable. But at least it's truthful.

It's easier to make socially acceptable excuses than to admit
your vulnerability and own up to what you're feeling. I know, you're
expected just to pull it together, put on your game face, and figure
it out no matter what happens. And, heaven forbid, anyone ever
know that you're struggling!

I know how fragile you are. I know the *real* you underneath the
"*I've got it all figured out*" façade. I know that sometimes you get
knocked down and feel utterly broken—like shattered (emotionally)
into a million pieces. And I know that every time you get knocked
down, you pick yourself back up, glue yourself back together and
keep going. I know because I do it too. We all do. We're resilient
like that!

Imagine yourself as a beautiful vase. (Of the priceless heirloom
variety, passed down for generations.) You've been through a lot!
You've been dropped, many times, sometimes without a crack,
and other times you've been shattered into pieces. And each time,
you've been glued back together. You've even been repainted a
couple of times so that on the outside, you look brand new. But on
the inside, you're a mess. You know that even the slightest bit of
pressure could cause you to crack all over again.

The excuses you're using are like cheap glue. They are a sad
attempt at preventing anyone from seeing how broken you perceive
yourself to be.

Even though you've done one heck of a job making yourself
appear "put together" (you get a new haircut, buy a beautiful

home, have a couple of great kids, achieve yet another business accomplishment), on the inside you still feel weak and fragile and on the verge of breaking. I know because, again, I've been there too. Here's the problem with that though: If we never fix the damage and correct the thoughts that are making us feel broken in the first place, we'll keep making excuses to stay in our safety zone. We'll keep playing small. And we'll continue to feel perpetually broken.

The excuses we make continue to reinforce our brain's negative patterns. They continue to feed the brain proof that we can't have the life we want. *"I can't start a business because I don't have enough time."* And the brain says, *"See! I was right. She's not good enough to balance a business and a life at the same time."*

So why do we make excuses? Because of fear of the past. What? Don't you mean fear of the future? Nope.

We can't fear something we haven't yet experienced. In order to fear something, we have to be able to imagine it. In order to imagine something, we have to rely on memories that help us create the story in our minds.

So what happens is that when we make excuses for not going after our dreams, what we're really doing is remembering an experience in which we tried something new and got a bad result.

Maybe you tried something new and were laughed at. Ridiculed. Judged. Maybe someone in your life disapproved of your choice and turned their back on you, leaving you feeling abandoned. Maybe your choice turned out differently than you imagined, and as a result, left you dealing with unpleasant consequences. Whatever happened, you associate the idea of taking a risk on yourself with negative emotions. And those emotions surface every time you start to think about taking a risk to improve your future.

The crazy part about recalling past painful memories is that our subconscious has no concept of time. It can't tell the difference between a real event and an imagined event or memory. So when we recall that memory, our brain releases the chemicals that cause us to feel that same emotional pain as if the event is happening in real time.

Why do you think you can get as worked-up about something today as when it happened five years ago? It's like you're right back there again. All of those emotions are all right there, bubbling over. This quality is really handy for actors. When they need to summon up real tears all they have to do it recall a painful memory of their past. And viola! Real tears. Because their brain truly believes that it's happening in real time. As I said, a handy tool for actors, but it's not all that helpful for anyone else.

In an attempt to protect us from reliving that pain over and over again (because who wants that, right?) our subconscious finds ways to protect us from any situation or experience that resembles that original experience that caused the pain in the first place. Enter self-sabotage, disguised as big, fat excuses.

I'm guessing you probably want to stop reliving that pain over and over again, right? Let's heal the hurt and move forward.

Let go of the story you've been telling yourself. Forgive yourself for your past. Sift through those painful memories and find the beautiful lessons within them. Those experiences are what made you the awesome, badass, go-getter that you are today! Love yourself for all you been through and everything you are. Abandon the excuses you've been making. And commit to doing the real work of healing.

Three months after my fifteenth birthday, my Dad kicked me

out of the house. Remember how I told you that my mom was doing drugs? Well, once it became apparent that my mom was dealing with an addiction, my Dad took custody of my sister and I. That lasted a whopping nine months before an argument (over I don't even remember what!) resulted in him throwing me out of his house.

My options were . . .

**A:** Live with my mom in a hotel room and risk having anything on my body that was even remotely valuable confiscated for drug money or,

**B:** Live on the streets.

I bounced back and forth between options, but mostly I chose B. Trust me, I relived the painful emotions I experienced that summer over and over again for years. As the days stretched on, I kept wondering if my Dad was going to call. I kept wondering, *"Did he care? Was he concerned that his daughter was running the streets, going to bars and after-hours raves? Sleeping on strangers' couches? Did he care if I was dead or alive?"*

Feeling abandoned and rejected by your parents is pretty painful stuff at any age, but at 15 it was particularly difficult. I allowed that pain to tear me up again and again for years until I decided I was done allowing myself to feel that way.

You cannot feel pain without a pain-inducing thought. To feel sad, you must think a sad thought. Otherwise, your brain will not release the chemicals that it takes to make you feel that way. You can't be nervous without first thinking a nervous thought. And you can't feel abandoned and rejected without thinking thoughts that provoke it.

Can you just numb the pain by not thinking at all? Sure, you can. I did that too, but when you do that, you become a walking zombie, numb to just about everything.

Instead of not thinking about that summer at all, I decided to think about it differently. I searched and searched within myself to find the silver lining and the positive parts of me that came from that experience.

Because of that summer, I am quite the badass! I have street smarts like you wouldn't believe. I learned a ton about how to read people's body language, expressions, and energy (very useful in business situations by the way, and especially handy in coaching!). I am resourceful, self-sufficient, and independent. Oh, and I learned how to rap, which comes in handy during karaoke night. I managed to turn the hurt and anger into appreciation. Because of that, I was able to summon compassion, empathy, and forgiveness toward my Dad—he is not a bad person just because he made a bad decision. He was doing the best he could with the emotions he was feeling at the time.

After working on seeing it from a broader perspective, and I am now grateful for that time in my life because those experiences empowered me to be the woman I am today. Without having gone through what I did, I wouldn't be able to empathize with my clients when they share stories of feeling rejected, abandoned, and not good enough. My experience has made me a stronger woman and a better coach. Without acknowledging the thoughts that created the feelings, though, I would never have been able to create that transformation in my life.

I'm not unique in my experience of turning an undesirable situation into a learning experience and source of strength. One of my clients, Alexa, has done the same, just like so many women I've been privileged to know, love, and work with.

Here's Alexa's inspiring story of loss and strength:

The pregnancy was high risk. We knew that it would be tough. But what came after giving birth to our twin girls, no one could have ever prepared us for. We lost Kathryn two days after she was born and spent 84 days in the NICU with Charis, praying that she'd survive.

It was such a whirlwind of emotion. Losing a child is traumatic. I replayed those early days in my mind again and again for years. Feeling a constant pull between grief over losing one child, and joy and gratitude for the life of the other, then guilt over feeling joy, then back to grief.

It was the saddest day of our lives. Without a doubt. But certainly, it had to be more than that. Kathryn's death had to be more than a sad day. It had to mean something. Be part of a purpose.

I started writing to sort through my feelings. Then, I published a blog. I thought, if I'm feeling this way—struggling with the loss of a child—then there had to be other parents who were in this same place. Maybe, just maybe, my words can help those who are grieving but also help people understand how to approach and talk to a grieving parent after they've lost a child.

Writing helped me declutter my toxic emotions. Thinking the same thoughts over and over was keeping me in a dark place—a place I risked being stuck in forever. But I knew that I had to move on, for myself and for my daughter who needed me.

I used the words that I wrote to help me find peace. To help me sort through the chaos that I was feeling. To give myself permission to choose a different path. To choose to be happy and still remember and honor my daughter, Kathryn.

I **chose** how I would reflect on what happened. I **chose** to find joy and honor her in a happy way.

I see her face every day when I look at her identical twin sister. And that brings me joy. We keep mementos all over the house that remind us of her. Sometimes they make me cry. And other times they bring me joy. Either way, it's a choice. Sometimes I need to go back there. I need to feel the sadness. And that's okay. I allow myself that space. Other times, I need to focus on life and what's right here in front of me at this moment. And that's okay too. When I need a little extra help getting to joy, I reach out and connect with people who make me laugh. I keep mantras on my wall and say them out loud. I take intentional action to connect me with things that I know will lift me up.

I've learned that the way we describe a situation determines how we think and feel about it.

We can choose to focus on the sadness and the pain. Or we can choose to find the beauty and joy. Sometimes it's difficult to do, trust me, I know. But it makes all the difference in the quality of your life going forward. If you can find the joy, if you raise yourself up and tap into better feeling emotions, you'll live a much healthier and abundant life.

How do we consciously change our choices, though? By digging deep into that in the workbook at the back of this book! But, for now, let me give you a little something now for you to take action on right away.

First, here's a quick reminder about the Law of Vibration. Everything in the universe has a vibration. At one end of the spectrum is positive or lighter vibration, and at the other end is negative and heavier vibration. And you know, there's a bunch in between because that's how spectrums work.

Emotions also have a vibration. You know when there's just something about someone that either draws you in or repels you? That's their vibration. That's why we say we like or don't like someone's "vibe."

So, negative emotions (like fear, anxiety, despair) are on the "low vibe" end of the spectrum while positive emotions (like joy, appreciation, empowerment) are on the "high vibe" end of the spectrum. Plus, there are a bunch of in-between emotions like hopefulness, boredom, anger, and more.

# EMOTIONAL *scale*

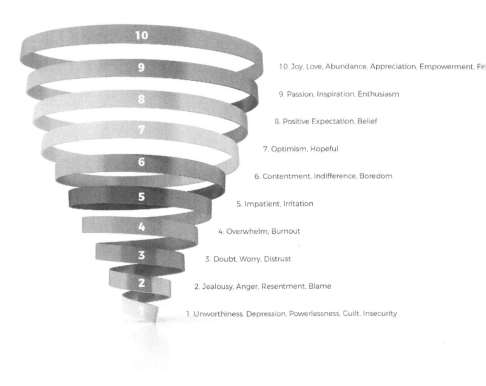

10. Joy, Love, Abundance, Appreciation, Empowerment, Fr

9. Passion, Inspiration, Enthusiasm

8. Positive Expectation, Belief

7. Optimism, Hopeful

6. Contentment, Indifference, Boredom

5. Impatient, Irritation

4. Overwhelm, Burnout

3. Doubt, Worry, Distrust

2. Jealousy, Anger, Resentment, Blame

1. Unworthiness, Depression, Powerlessness, Guilt, Insecurity

*This scale was adapted from the Emotional Guidance Scale used famously by the teachings of Abraham. I've simplified it for my personal use in coaching. If you'd like to learn more about the scale as well as additional exercises that will help you align with a higher vibrational frequency, I recommend reading: Ask and It Is Given by Esther and Jerry Hicks*

How can you make this scale work to your benefit? Well, what most people do when they find themselves experiencing a low-vibe emotion is try to get as high on the scale as possible. And they inevitably fail because it doesn't work like that. It's like trying to jump from the bottom of a staircase, straight to the top. Not going to happen. You have two options: take it one stair at a time, or take bigger steps and skip a stair or two. Either way, you're climbing the stairs in increments. Not all at once.

Likewise, you're improving your emotional state one incremental step at a time. You're not going to go from despair to joy in 30 seconds. You have to hit the steps in between and work your way up.

If, for example, you're feeling "worried" (#3) about something, you can move yourself up by two steps to "irritated" (#5) a whole lot easier than you can move yourself up to "enthusiasm" (#9). And you can do that simply and easily by changing your thoughts.

The overall idea is that you are capable of altering your feelings, getting yourself in a better emotional state, and controlling your vibration.

Just like you can be aware of, and change your words, and monitor and alter your thoughts, you can also check in with and adjust your feelings. That means you can slow down and eventually stop the bad feelings from taking over. The workbook in the back of this book will walk you through the process of making this happen. Remember, you are in control! Decide how you want to feel, then begin the work to raise your emotional state until you're in vibrational alignment with what you desire for yourself.

For instance, if you want more joy, love, and abundance in your life, you must first align yourself with that vibration by feeling those emotions. You'd do this by speaking words, focusing your thoughts and engaging in activities that elicit these emotions. Once you are immersed in feelings of joy, love, and abundance, you'll begin to attract things into your life that reinforce those emotions and help you to sustain that vibration.

# Chapter 10
# Beliefs Layer

Buried deep in the subconscious mind—below our words, thoughts, and feelings—is the layer that holds the most power: Beliefs. Technically, it's not even a layer; It's the core. That's why they're often referred to as *core beliefs*.

When we learn how to shift our beliefs, that's when the real mindset magic happens. It becomes a million times easier to speak about yourself in a healthy way; talk about your dreams with a knowing that your desires are on their way to you; your thoughts become abundant and upbeat; your feelings will continue to fluctuate but will mostly be rooted in love, joy, and happiness. And your positive beliefs about yourself, the world, life and what's possible will continue to get stronger.

Shifting your beliefs, though, takes time. That's because what you want to believe and what you *actually* believe may be totally different things. You may want to believe that all people are inherently good, but if you watch the news and subconsciously label some people and behaviors as evil, then what you want to believe and what you actually believe are not the same thing.

You may want to believe that *"all you need is love,"* but if you argue with your spouse about things like money and household chores, then that's not really what you believe.

Sit with that for a moment, because this is where we dig deep and get honest with ourselves about what we *really* believe to be true.

Disempowering beliefs are what create the limits in your life, and empowering beliefs are what remove those limits. When you shift your focus from what you cannot do and instead choose to focus on what you can do, your life will become limitless.

It's time to declutter and let go of your limits. First, you need to become aware of the disempowering beliefs that you're currently holding onto. Then we will work on replacing those disempowering beliefs with empowering words, thoughts, and feelings. And once you start to experience the world in a different way—through this new positivity filter—and see the proof that something amazing can be true for you, your beliefs will change as a result.

First, you do need to work through the other layers– words, thoughts, and feelings. Unfortunately, you can't just wake up and think, *"I'm going to believe something different today!"* If it were that easy, you wouldn't be reading this book (and I wouldn't have a reason to write it).

Even if something does seem to change in a moment, it's so easy to slip back into your old, comfortable (yet disempowering) belief system. It took a lot of years to solidify that belief inside of you, and it's going to take time for those deeply rooted limits to surface and dissipate. Rome wasn't built in a day, and the same is true of your limiting language, thought patterns and default emotions. So, it's only fair that I warn you: they aren't going to transform in a day either. But they will transform if you follow the steps and do the work. I promise!

Where do beliefs come from, anyway? Well, beliefs usually come from one of three places:

# Childhood

We are taught a *lot* of things very early in life. Much of what we're taught isn't even explicit. Rather, it comes in the form of attitudes or comments or the general energy surrounding a topic. Those seemingly benign experiences become rooted in how we see the world.

How many times did you hear growing up that "money doesn't grow on trees." What do those words really mean? At the time this phrase meant that money was scarce and because money was scarce you couldn't have the new jeans all the other kids were wearing, so you had to show up to school in last year's "uncool" jeans, feeling like an outsider, while wondering if everyone was secretly making fun of your outdated look.

See what *really* happened there? Your brain linked up the pattern: Money = Scarcity = Emotional Pain. You created a belief that money (or lack of money) is painful. You might, to this day, live in a state of scarcity and fear around not having enough money, just from one painful little memory.

How about "to love is to sacrifice." Did you grow up in a household where sacrifice was made in the name of love? Perhaps your mother chose to give up her career to stay home and raise you and your siblings. You felt torn between feelings of guilt that she had to make such a sacrifice, selfish joy because you got to keep her all to yourself, and gratitude that she was there. You want the people in your life to know you love them as much as your mom loved you. You've learned (subconsciously) that if you love someone, you should put their needs before your own. You now find yourself choosing between your goals and doing what's "right" in the name of service and love. You may never even stop to think, *"Do I really have to choose? Can't I have both?"* Because of your belief system, that's not how your brain was wired to think.

Did the people in your life growing up work hard? Did they value a hard day's work? You perhaps heard the words "no pain, no gain" more times than you can count, and watched as the adults around you were praised for trading their time, mental health, and physical well-being for money. You can remember times when you worked really hard on something and received praise and recognition from your parents for the dedication and rigorous effort you put forth. *That felt good.* There were times, however, when you were especially proud of yourself for doing something that came easy. You couldn't wait to show it off and get that lavish praise. Instead, you got a half-baked, *"Good job, honey,"* and you were defeated. It reinforced the belief that Hard Work + Pain = Praise (pleasure). And that Easy = Disappointment + Pain. If this is a belief you hold, you can bet your ass that it's manifesting in (and sabotaging) your life in various ways. Do you find yourself working harder than everyone else at the same job? Over-delivering? Going above and beyond until you experience burnout? Do you believe that the one who works the hardest will get the furthest? Yep. That's a result of believing that you have to work hard to be seen as successful.

How many other mantras can you recall hearing growing up? How did these words manipulate your thoughts and emotions when you were a child? How have these experiences become the truths that influence your experience of the world today?

These aren't objective truths, of course, but when we hear them in childhood and don't know anything different, we accept them as truths. It's our responsibility as adults to recognize them, expose them, and recreate them.

## Repetition

While many of our deeply rooted beliefs were created in our

formative years, that doesn't mean we are immune to limiting beliefs sneaking their way into our subconscious now that we're grown. It can (and does) happen all the time!

That's because when we are exposed to a statement or message enough times, it becomes too hard to ignore (remember the milk example in chapter 6?). Our brain, that is trying like mad to filter out the nonessential information that gets thrown at us all day, gets too tired to resist it, and so it starts to look for "proof" in the world around us that will help it to confidently label the information as "true" or "untrue" (important or unimportant). When we start to see proof (or what looks like proof), the neurons in the brain make a connection. The more proof we find, the stronger those connections become. Before you know it, that connection gets rooted in our minds as a solid belief.

*"Marriage is hard work."*

Take, for instance, the statement: *"Marriage is hard work."* You might not believe this the first time you hear it. You might even blatantly disagree with it. Until, you start to notice how all your married friends constantly complain about their struggle to keep the marriage alive. Your brain says, *"That looks like proof to me,"* and Bam! A neural connection is made. Then, your neighbor, who you thought was happily married, tells you she's getting a divorce. (More proof.) You start to notice billboards everywhere advertising divorce lawyers. You think back to all the people you know and realize that more people in your life are divorced than married, and those who are married aren't all that happy. And Boom! Just like that: Your brain labels "marriage is hard work" as truth, and a new belief is formed.

*"You can relax when you retire."*

Are you watching the people around you work their asses off

and never take a vacation? They won't stop climbing that ladder until they hit the ceiling or die—whichever comes first. After all, we've got to keep up with the Joneses, right? The people in your life are goal-driven and success-oriented. That is if you define success is all work and no play. Your inner circle consists of people who believe relaxation is something that is earned only after you have done all the things you're "supposed" to do: Buy a nice home, a fancy car, pay for your kids' college education, and fund your retirement account. After all, that's what everyone has done your whole life. So you scrimp, and you save, and you sacrifice. You work evenings, weekends and holidays, all so you can have all the things you're supposed to have. You find yourself counting down the days until you retire and finally start to enjoy your life. Why? Because that's also what the people around you do. That's what they've always done. It's been repeated so many times, that, now, it has become your own deeply rooted belief system that says: *"That's just how it works."*

*"You can't trust people."*

Growing up, my Dad used to play the game "Trust me" with my younger sister and I. He'd hold out his arms, and we'd have to stay stiff as a board and fall backward into his arms. If we trusted him, we'd stay straight. If we didn't trust him, we'd bend our knees and fall on our butts. Well, to prove his point, "Never trust anybody" he'd routinely move his arms and let us fall (there was always a pillow there). I think it was his strange way of teaching his daughters to be independent and cautious. Over the years I experienced many situations that offered "proof" that he was right. At 13, I had everything I owned taken away from me and given to another teenage girl—my clothes, bedroom furniture, stereo equipment and cd's, everything. At 15, my mom would take any cash or valuables I had on me to buy drugs. At age 16, my boyfriend cheated on me (then almost every boyfriend after that cheated on me). By the time I was an adult, I had accumulated so much proof that "You can't trust people" it had become a solidified belief. I'm sure you can imagine what kinds of limits that belief created for me. It took some work, but thanks to the **Mindset Switch System**, I was able to flip the switch and begin to trust people again.

All of these are common limiting beliefs. We hear them over and over in our culture, and we see enough people who go through these experiences that the overwhelming repetition looks a lot like "evidence," and so we accept it as truth.

## Traumatic experiences

Anytime something outside of the ordinary happens in our lives, it leaves an impact on our emotions and our brain. Any experience that has jolted you or shook you to your core has the opportunity to create a limiting belief. When you lose a job, lose someone you love, go through a devastating breakup or divorce, experience abuse, witness something horrific, or become the victim of betrayal, your faith in humanity, people, and the world becomes tainted. All of these experiences have the potential to create a negative belief. They don't have to, though. Even the most traumatic experiences can reinforce positive beliefs.

Trust me, I've been there! I shared with you a few of my childhood experiences. I lost my mom to drug addiction, was kicked out of my house, spent an entire summer homeless, became a teen mom—I'm no stranger to trauma. I can tell you with complete sincerity, though, I don't regret a single experience. Sounds crazy, I know. But I believe that everything happens for a reason. Those experiences made me the strong, independent, resourceful, determined, compassionate woman I am today. And they are the fuel behind my life mission of empowering others to find their own strength and take charge of their life in a way that leaves nothing up to chance. If I had not had those experiences, what motivation would I have to write this book? Would I be as passionate about what I do? About helping others stand in their power and show up in the world in impactful ways? I can't be sure. But I doubt it.

I'm a huge fan of Tony Robbins, so when his documentary, *I am Not Your Guru* came out, I couldn't wait to watch it. The film features an intervention Tony has with Dawn Watson, a suicidal 26-year-old woman who, at first glance seems to have the world at her feet—she's gorgeous, well-dressed, and educated. Upon first glance, you might have thought she had an unshakable confidence about her. That is until she shared her story of why she was contemplating taking her own life. She was raised in a community called the *Children of God* where they believed that God's love was shared with others through sex. Where young girls and boys, beginning at the age of six, were being sexually abused in the name of God. And there was no way out. She had spent her entire life being abused herself and also watching her mother, brother, and friends get abused. She felt powerless to do anything to stop it. Dawn was tired of being the strong one who was holding her family together. She was tired of carrying around the emotional pain she had been burdened with for so many years. She believed that, although she wanted a better life for herself and her family, that there were no options available to her. She felt powerless to help herself or her family.

Tony helped her break through her limiting belief patterns and *flip the switch*. He helped her to shift her focus away from what had happened and instead focus on what was possible. He helped her find the tiny thread of a silver lining. He helped her to see, right in that room in front of hundreds of people, that love did exist and that she did have a choice. She could choose to stop the abuse and use the strength that she had gained as a result of surviving such trauma, to help other people overcome their own struggles. He helped her see that, as a survivor, she had a tremendous gift.

Dawn is now helping people all over the world overcome abusive situations. Yes, Tony Robbins is freaking amazing! But he didn't perform a miracle. He only helped her switch her focus.

The good news is that you can do this too. You don't need Tony Robbins or me or any other guru for that matter. You only need to ask yourself the questions that will put you back in the driver's seat of your own life and will help you concentrate your focus on the positive aspects and possibilities.

When we set out to change our lives, we tend to put conditions on our big dreams. We set up our dreams in an "if this, then that" format.

We tell ourselves that "XYZ" has to happen in order to be happy, deserving, joyful, and relaxed.

*If I ever find my soulmate, then I'll be happy.*
*If I retire comfortably, then I'll get to relax.*
*If I hit the 6-figure mark in my business, then I'll be successful.*

When you set goals in this way what you're implying is that you don't feel like you're enough or that you're worthy. You believe that you have to go through hell to get to heaven.

But that's not true and, deep down, you know it!

How many times have you thought about something you want and thought that you have to earn it first? In your work or business?

In your love life? In friendship? In your family?

What do you have to do to earn the right to feel successful and abundant? When will you earn the right to feel carefree and happy?

Let me tell you something: You've already earned the right to these things; you're breathing.

Everyone deserves to be happy. And by that, I don't mean just content. I mean blissfully, ecstatically, dancing on cloud nine, in love with life, singing from the mountain tops, happy!

Today. Right now. No. Matter. What.

And if you don't believe that, that's where you need to start. If you don't believe that you deserve (right this second) your Dream Life, that belief is rooted in a feeling of unworthiness.

## Unworthiness is the root cause of all other blocks.

What is it that you want? What makes up your Dream Life? Go ahead and list it out. Take a moment to do a Dream Life brain dump.

Now, what's stopping you from having it right now? List out all the reasons why you can't have that today. (You can get started on this right now, by turning to the *Pinpoint, Purge and Prove* exercise in the Declutter section of the Workbook.)

Those reasons are what's blocking you. All the excuses—I'm too old, too young, too skinny, too fat, too blonde, too whatever. I don't have enough education, enough time, enough money, I'm not an expert, not skilled enough, not as good as this other person. (Yeah, I've heard them all!)

All of those excuses (or "reasons" if you want to keep calling them that for now) are just your negative beliefs talking. And none of them are actually true.

What are these excuses really saying? I'm not enough right now. I'm not worthy.

If you believe that you have to put in your time, work hard, and sacrifice for your dreams to come true, or if you believe that you're unable to realize your dreams because you lack some secret ingredient (skill, time, economic status, experience, support, etc.), I have a few more questions for you: What would happen if you could have it all now? Right this minute? What if those limits didn't exist? What if your dream life was available to you right now? Would grabbing ahold of your dreams and taking what's available for you make you selfish, greedy, entitled? Would you lose someone you love? Would you have to risk something important? Sacrifice something you value? What's the worst that could happen?

## What if you believed something different?

What if you believed:

*I am enough.*
*I am lovable.*
*I am valuable.*
*I am worthy.*
*I am strong.*
*I am independent*
*I am capable.*
*I am safe.*
*I am in control.*
*I'm an amazing parent.*
*I'm an incredible lover.*
*I'm an awesome friend.*
*I am worthy of support.*
*I am worthy of love.*

*I am worthy of friendship.*
*I am worth it. Whatever "it" may be.*

If these statements don't feel true – WHY? What thoughts come up that challenge this truth? Those thoughts are pointing directly toward your limiting belief(s). Did you immediately think of a negatively-charged experience where you didn't feel that way? Ok, good. Awareness is step one. Now, think of a positive memory or experience that you've had where you did feel that way. And then, think of another. Sometimes our brains just need to be reminded that the positive affirmations we want to believe are already true.

Braffirmations are a wonderful tool to use here too! (Refer back to chapter 5 for an in-depth explanation of how to construct a braffirmation.)

What else do you need to say, think and feel for these statements to be true for you? What can you do to gather more "proof" so that they feel authentic and genuine?

These transformations aren't going to happen in an hour. It takes work when it's a deeply rooted limit. Trust me, if I could wave a magic wand and transform everyone's limiting beliefs into rockstar-level empowering beliefs, I would. But we all need to put in a little conscious effort if we want to flip the switch.

A client of mine, Tara, had some common negative beliefs when we started working together. Most of them centered around beliefs such as, *"My expertise can't possibly be enough for people to pay me,"* and *"You have to work hard and struggle before you succeed."*

When she started her copywriting business, she had a tough time charging clients what she was worth because of these limiting beliefs. She sent out an invoice for $15 for a piece of written copy to one of her clients. That's where I had to draw a line in the sand and talk her through some of her blocks.

Because she was new in business, she believed that she didn't have the experience or expertise to charge more. Because she wouldn't pay high prices for writing services, she believed others wouldn't pay a higher price. Because she grew up around a family who struggled and valued a strong work ethic, she believed building a thriving business had to be hard, that she had to pay her dues and that she had to struggle before really seeing the payoff.

When I coached her through all that and helped her realize that none of that is actually true, she was able to transform her limiting beliefs into empowering ones.

*I have the expertise to charge a premium price.*
*I can build a thriving business with ease.*

And she did. And her business continues to grow.

Unfortunately, you can't change your beliefs the way you can change your words, thoughts or even your feelings. But you can transform your beliefs by tweaking the other layers first.

One of the most impactful questions you can ask to get that process started is: What do I need to let go of?

That could be a person, something about your environment, defeating language, disempowering thoughts, negative self-talk, or the meaning you're giving to an experience in your life. You might think some of these things are outside of your control, but, I'm willing to bet you have more control over them than you realize.

External circumstances, for instance, are one of those things you don't have total control over. And while they are not the "be all, end all" of what your life can look like, the way you respond to them does make a difference. You can't always control the events themselves, but you can control what meaning you attach to them. And by doing that, you can control what happens in your life from there.

Remember those sisters I mentioned before? There are some gut-level fundamental beliefs at play there. At the core of what they believe about themselves based on their (almost identical) life experiences is this:

First sister: *"I'm not worthy. I'm just here for other people to use me."*

Second sister: *"I survive and rise above."*

See the difference? They experienced the same kind of trauma. But how they each responded to their experience is astoundingly different—and something they each have total control over, always. This means that the first sister can still make that change if she chooses to. That choice is always available.

Choice is always available to you, too. Right now. In this moment. Everything in your life has led you here. Not only "here" in your life experiences, but "here" in picking up this book. And reading this far. And taking a peek or two at the workbook. And then . . . Doing. The. Work.

You are rewriting your own life story. All the negative self-talk and demeaning thoughts and feelings that settle themselves into a belief system that says you aren't good enough? You're changing all of that right now at this moment.

This is powerful stuff. You are making a choice to take control and make things different. You are steering in the direction of empowerment, freedom, true happiness, and abundance. Your time is now!

When we are closed-minded and pretend to know what is (and what is not) possible for us, what we're really doing is building walls that keep us contained within the reality that is familiar to us. We are creating our own limitations.

# Chapter 11
## The Mindset Switch System

Congratulations! You're now ready for the action-step you've been waiting for. (And if you skipped to this part, and you want to achieve the best results possible, I strongly suggest that you read all the previous chapters, especially the ones on layers, first!)

When I started learning about how powerfully transformative mindset work could be, I remember thinking, *"This is great, but now what? Where's the action plan? How can I actually use this?"* When I was first reading and researching, there was a lot of advice and books that resonated with me, for sure. But one thing didn't: there was no system. Nothing that was repeatable. Nothing I could implement again and again with predictable results. I needed that in my life. Time is too precious to waste on experiments. I wanted something that worked fast! And there was nothing like that.

So I did the only thing I could do; I experimented anyway. And after years of testing (and getting consistent results), I created the **Mindset Switch System**. For myself, yes, but more importantly for you and everyone who is just like us. People who know that they have potential inside of them; who know there is more out there in the world for them and who want to unleash the possibilities of all that awaits them—not later, but now!

This system is designed to guide you through taking action and making some serious changes in your life. It's not necessarily an ordered process, as you may find yourself wanting to repeat a step a few times as you are working through the layers of your personal transformation. It will, however, serve as a guide as you embark on the transformative journey of changing your mindset.

I've created this system from the countless psychology and mindset-related materials (books, courses, movies, research papers, etc.) I've studied over the last decade. It's my signature blend of what I like to call "practical woo": a mix of woo-woo and rational practicality. It's my useful, realistic way of implementing all of my favorite woo-woo tricks. It's a combination of everything I've read from Abraham Hicks, Tony Robbins, Gabby Bernstein, Deepak Chopra, The Secret, Joe Dispenza, Brené Brown, Carol Dweck, quantum physics, behavioral psych, neuro-linguistic programming, Jack Canfield, Dale Carnegie, Louise Hay . . . and so many more! (Yeah, we're on a first-name basis over at my local library!)

If you don't like the results you've been getting and you want (or need!) something different, the Mindset Switch System will guide you through how to do it.

**The Mindset Switch System:** The 5-step action plan that will transform your life!


- DISCOVER
- DREAM
- DECLUTTER
- DO (SOMETHING!)
- DETACH

First, let me break each piece of the system down and explain what it means so you can learn how to activate it and start making it work for you. I'm giving you the overview here, but make sure to also check out the workbook in part 2 of this book to dig deep into some activities that will have a significant impact on helping you work through this system and flip the switch!

## DISCOVER

What isn't working in your life right now? The purpose of the Discover process is to dig in and figure out what you don't want. What isn't serving you anymore? What is driving you batshit crazy right now? You know, those things that keep happening that leave you thinking, "*This sucks. This isn't what I want!*"

Most personal development texts would prefer to have you focus on only the positive, with an emphasis on gratitude, appreciation and celebrating the present moment (we'll get to all that). In my experience though, those practices are like trying to cure cancer with cold medicine. Sometimes addressing the symptom isn't enough. Sometimes you have to run some tests, diagnose and treat the underlying problem.

Most people avoid digging into the Discover process because they are afraid of learning the truth about what's really causing their unhappiness, and then feeling obligated to do something about it. So they adopt the "ignorance is bliss" mentality and they choose to ignore the fact that something is wrong. And guess what happens? That's right! Nothing!

The Discover process of the Mindset Switch System can be the most vulnerable and sometimes painful step because it means you have to go inside yourself and be willing to seek truth, but it will give you some impactful answers and point you in the direction you want to go.

Discovering your personal truth requires you to reconnect with yourself, and your intuition. All of the answers you seek, all of the guidance you long for, all the clarity in the world is already within you. All you have to do is pay attention. Meditation is the most effective way that I've found to do this. It's simply a matter of shutting off your mind. I know that sounds hard, and at first, it is. Like, really hard. But it gets easier with practice. I suggest finding a meditation practice that works for you; something that helps you still your mind and reconnect with yourself. That may mean a traditional meditation pose (sitting with your eyes closed and "ohm-ing," but it doesn't have to). It can mean going on long quiet walks by yourself or simply relaxing in the bathtub. Journaling is another excellent way to tune into your thoughts and feelings. Anything that allows you to do careful observing and slow down enough to be aware.

Other powerful tools to help you reconnect with yourself during the Discover process are: Oracle Cards, using a Pendulum, journaling, hypnosis, talking to a trusted friend, coach, therapist, or intuitive.

## DREAM

This is the fun part! You get to let your imagination run wild, dream big about what you want and get super clear about what that means for you.

If you've gone through the Discover process, you already know what you don't want. Which means you can pretty easily pinpoint what you do want for your life, just by identifying the opposite.

Remember, dreaming is different than goal-setting. Goals are actionable, but they aren't based on what we want at our core and why we want them. Sure, you can say *"I wanna make $10k* *a month,*" but it's easy to miss why you want that and to identify *what it will mean for you.* With goal-setting, we it's easy to get too attached to the "how" and let those negative voices try to convince us it's impossible (or we set the bar too high) because, well, let's face it, it can get hard.

When you're clear about the deeply rooted desire, the "why" behind what it is that you want, the desire itself suddenly becomes stronger than the risk. And when that happens, nothing will stop you! During the Dream phase, you are getting clear on what you want, emotionally connecting to your why, and fueling that desire.

## Getting Started with DREAM

Many folks will tell you to shoot for the stars and to set wildly audacious, hairy scary goals, and go for your wildest dreams right out of the gate. Not me. I've seen too many people, high on an energy buzz after attending a seminar or reading a personal development book, allow themselves to set a dream so big that once the buzz wore off, they felt even further away from their dream than they did before they attended the seminar or read the book.

Don't misunderstand. I want you to dream big and go for everything you've ever wanted, and then some! But what I want for you even more than to go for your dreams is for you to actually *make them happen!*

If you're not experienced in visualizing (and believing in) a life that is way beyond your current zone of familiarity, you might want to start by allowing yourself to stretch your imagination just a little bit at first, and then, incrementally, push yourself to dream bigger once you've proven to yourself that it's possible and safe to do so.

Start with a dream that feels lofty but attainable. It should feel slightly uncomfortable, yet exciting at the same time.

For example, if you've always dreamed of traveling and exploring the world, but you've never even stepped foot out of your hometown, the thought of traveling halfway around the world might seem impossible. Sure, it sounds great in theory, but there are all those unknowns. *"I don't speak the language." "What about terrorists?" "I don't even have a passport." "Where will I stay?" "It's dangerous to travel alone." "What will I do with my time?"* And before you know it, you've talked yourself right out of going for it.

Here's what you do instead: Start by planning a weekend trip that is just 4 hours away. After spending two days by yourself and discovering that you can, in fact, find plenty to do, it is safe, and it's easier than you originally thought, you'll feel more confident about allowing yourself to dream a little bigger. Next time, dreaming up a trip that is a short plane ride away. After a little practice, your brain runs out of excuses and is willing to get on board with any dream you can possibly whip up.

As kids, we're really good at going for the big lofty dream right out of the gate, but have since let our dreams shrink down to what society tells us is reasonable. We let the world tell us that our dreams aren't realistic, that we can minimize disappointment by lowering our expectations of what we can accomplish or have. And so, we listen. And what do we get? A half-assed version of what we really want!

No more, my friend. Your dreams are not only yours by birthright; they are waiting for you to seize them. But first, you have to identify what they are.

A great way to get clear on your dreams and desires is to visualize what your ideal life could look like. Again, this doesn't have to be so lofty that it feels unattainable. Try visualizing your perfect life in six months, one year or three years. Close your eyes and let your imagination fill in the details. What are you doing? Where are you living/ working? Who is in your life? How are you spending your time? How do you feel? Then, take that one step further by designing a vision board that represents everything you imagined for yourself in that visualization.

Look at that vision board every day. Those are the intentions you're putting into the Universe. And those, my friend, are the things that you have the power to create!

All you have to do is believe it's possible.

If, at this point, you're thinking: *"How do I do that? I want to believe that my dream life is possible but I have so many doubts. It's like there's a voice in my head arguing with me. As if my mind is calling B.S. on my dreams!"* You're not alone. Although most people love the act of dreaming and visualizing, the thought of actually realizing their dreams can feel far-fetched, which is why the next step is so important! It's where we declutter all the triggers, self-talk, thoughts, and feelings that are contributing to your limiting beliefs—the beliefs that try to convince you that that the life you dream of is anything but possible.

My favorite tools for use during the Dream phase are guided meditation, visualization, journaling, desire maps, and vision boards.

## DECLUTTER

This is where you get to get rid of everything that's not supporting your dream life vision. Ask yourself: *"On a scale of 1-10, what is my level of belief that my dreams are possible for me?"* (refer to the Emotional Scale to answer this question) If your answer is anything less than an 8, we've got some decluttering work to do!

What is causing you to question the possibilities? Identify it and get rid of it! You know all that stuff that makes you feel yucky/annoyed/guilty/etc.? Get rid of that too!

It might be your words, the people you spend time with, the things in your house that, when you look at them, make you feel like a second-class citizen. Literally, declutter anything and everything that is standing in the way of your absolute greatness. It's pretty easy to know how to get rid of physical items or even words, but what about feelings that you want to declutter? Forgiveness is the way to declutter those. The act of forgiveness and letting go of resentment or anger is like an emotional detox! It's just about as fun as a colon cleanse, but it can be super powerful and totally worth it.

**Getting Started with DECLUTTER**

First, identify what you need to declutter from your life and then make a commitment to work on one thing at a time. Remember, Rome wasn't built in a day. Start with the easy stuff—declutter the junk around your house, clean out some closets, give away the clothes that you know you'll never wear again.

Then, detox from the negativity in your environment. Take a break from watching the news (if it's important enough, you'll hear about it, trust me!). Does social media trigger you? What about the reverters, energy vampires, victims and negative protectors in your life? Give yourself permission to take a break from anything that drags your vibe down. It's just not worth it.

After you've worked through your triggers, you can begin to work on yourself. I recommend starting with your words. Begin by decluttering your negative self-talk. Play the Buzz Words for a week, a month or more. You might even want to start with decluttering one word or phrase at a time until it becomes habit. Then add more words and phrases to your Buzz Word List as you feel ready.

After you conquered your verbal dialogue, it's time to begin decluttering negative thoughts. You already know that I love affirmations (or mantras), and more specifically, braffirmations for this. Equally effective for refusing thoughts is practicing gratitude. Simply pausing throughout your day and allowing yourself to appreciate the many people, things, and experiences that bring you joy can be tremendously powerful in keeping your thoughts aligned with a positive, happy vibe.

To take back control over your emotions, what you'll want to do is slow yourself down several times a day and simply pay attention. How are you feeling? What thoughts are contributing to those feelings? Then choose a better, more empowering thought to focus on.

Another tool that I especially love to introduce my clients to during the decluttering process is Emotional Freedom Technique (EFT) or "tapping," which can be transformative for letting go of emotional baggage and negativity. Does it feel super weird to talk to yourself and tap parts of your body? Heck yeah. But trust me, it works!

(For an instructional video on EFT, go to www.tonyarineer. com/ms-bonuses)

## DO

DO - SOMETHING! Listen, nothing is going to change unless you take action. Yes, the Universe will do some amazing things for you, but you have to do your part. You have to meet the Universe halfway.

In my experience, the best way to show the Universe that you're serious about going after your dream life, and reinforcing to your brain that you're not willing to take "no" for an answer, is to commit to taking small, but consistent, action steps toward your dream.

This means doing something every single day that pushes you just a little bit outside of your comfort zone. Now, when I say small steps, I mean exactly that. The things you do shouldn't be terrifying, just a little uncomfortable.

For instance, if your dream is to be a world-renowned speaker, yet, the thought of speaking in public sends you into a full-blown anxiety attack, it doesn't make sense to start pitching conferences in an attempt to secure a keynote spot. That's just too big of a leap. What you *could* do, however, is commit to taking action steps that are smaller and only slightly scary rather than downright terrifying, but still move you toward your ultimate dream of being a speaker. Join a Toastmasters Club, record yourself giving a speech, go live on Facebook, host a webinar or in-person workshop, speak at a local Chamber of Commerce event.

Every time you push beyond your limits, you send a message to your brain that it is safe to try new things and that you are capable of succeeding at anything you put your mind to! It also results in increased feelings of empowerment, confidence, and faith in yourself and it raises your vibe, which tells the Universe *"I've totally got this! I'm ready for more opportunities like this. I'm ready to take action toward my dreams. I'm ready to take my life to the next level!"*

### Getting Started with DO:

What action steps should you take? Should I develop a complex strategy? Do I need to reverse engineer an action plan? Nope! I recommend keeping it super simple.

Take daily inspired action. No plan. No strategy. Just promise yourself that you'll do something every day. Then, each morning, allow yourself some space to determine what that something is.

Here's how it works:

You'll need to set aside a few minutes every morning to do this. First, go through your typical morning routine (If you don't already have a morning routine that you love, I suggest reading *Miracle Morning* by Hal Elrod). Then, before you being your normal day, spend a minute or two looking at your vision board, if you have one, or visualizing yourself living your dream life. Then, quiet your mind, and get into a relaxed, meditative state. Once you're relaxed, ask the question: *"What can I do today to move me closer to my dream life?"* Other variations of this question are *"What can I do to be of service today?"* or *"What can I do to connect to my desire of _____?"* And then, allow the answer to come to you.

Then, once you do the thing you felt inspired to do, make sure you celebrate! Do a happy dance, write about it in your journal, post a victory selfie on Instagram, brag about it on Facebook, treat yourself to a hot bath, a yoga session or a glass of wine. Enjoy the feeling of accomplishment. Stepping outside of your comfort zone (even if the step is small) is a HUGE accomplishment. It means that you felt the fear and you did it anyway. That requires courage, perseverance, conviction, and badassery. And above all else, it is a testament to how much you believe in yourself. And that is worth celebrating!

A fun tool that I love to introduce during this phase is Binaural Beats, which use brainwave frequencies by way of repetitive sounds and music to induce stress-relief, motivation, creativity, focus or relaxation. It's a handy little tool to get you over a hump so you can burst into action fast, and it's especially useful for emotional and spiritual healing.

Read, research, and immerse yourself in the practice of understanding different vibrations of emotions and master the art of choosing a higher vibe. (For an up-to-date list of all my favorite books, tools, and resources on all things vibration, manifesting, and attraction, visit www.tonyarineer.com/ms-resources)

## DETACH

This is the part of the process where we focus on the art of allowing things to happen, rather than forcing them to happen. If you're serious about getting what you want, you've got to learn to detach yourself from the outcome of the change you're trying to create. Ask yourself: "On a scale of 1-10, how detached am I from the outcome?" Again, if your answer is anything less than an 8, we've got work to do!

When you're too attached to something, your vibe goes way down. You become desperate, worried, fearful, anxious, and panicky. All those limiting words, thoughts, and feelings creep back in (and all the work you've done to get to this point goes out the window).

Try not to get attached to what you think it's supposed to look like, or how you think it's supposed to happen. Just open up, allow the Universe to surprise you, and have faith that it will happen. This requires the practice of faith and confidence, and is the hardest part for just about everybody I've ever worked with. We all want to be in control and be the action takers. We all want to know, with certainty, that we're going to get that thing we desire. But here's the crazy thing: Once you let go of the need to have it, that's when it will appear.

To get into the practice of letting go, ask yourself: *"If this it doesn't work out the way I expect, or when I want, so what? What will that mean? Will it really the end of the world? Or is there something better for me around the corner?"* I'm of the mindset that the Universe has something even bigger and better for you. When you embrace that mindset, too, you'll find that it's a whole lot easier to detach from the outcome and master the art of allowing.

When it comes to allowing, dogs are great teachers. I'm not kidding! They know they're going to eat, right? They don't try to plan and map out when and where their next meal is coming from. They just expect it to come. How many times have you heard someone say, *"When I die, I wanna come back as my dog!"* Why do you think they say that? Because dogs don't have a care in the world. They're not worried. They're not stressed out. They are able to just enjoy the moment . . . all the time. Think of detaching as channeling your inner dog. I know, it sounds weird, but you know what I mean.

Detaching is all about distracting yourself long enough to maintain the vibe you created in the do phase (where you took action and as a result felt freaking amazing!). And when you can maintain that feel-good vibe, that's the vibration in which dreams manifest and miracles happen!

At that point, everything becomes easy. Struggles go away, stress goes away, and it seems that no matter what, everything always seems to work out for the best.

### Getting Started with DETACH:

The key to detaching and allowing abundance to manifest in your life is self-awareness. Know what fills your cup, know what feels good and do it as often as possible (as long as it's safe and healthy, of course). If being in nature is what fuels your soul, make sure to schedule regular hikes or outside meditation time. Do you need to connect with friends to feel alive? Have a weekly fun night.

Whatever it takes to keeps your vibe up, do it!

Appreciation and gratitude (I told you we'd come back to this) are wonderful practices that will help you to maintain you high-vibe energy. Whether that means a daily prayer practice or starting a gratitude journal, implement something that makes you aware of all of the positive aspects of your life on a daily basis.

Remember, joyful activities don't have to be planned out in your calendar. Allowing yourself to be spontaneous is one of the best ways to keep your vibe high. Dancing in the car at a stop light, singing your favorite song when it pops into your head, compliment a stranger, do a cartwheel just because you feel like it, roll down a hill, climb a tree. Think back to the things you did as a child that brought you joy, and do more of that!

Follow the process outlined in the Mindset Switch System and your life will dramatically transform. I guarantee it! If you want to share your ah-ha moments and stories of personal transformation with me, email me anytime at: tonya@tonyarineer.com. I can't wait to hear from you!

## The Mindset Switch System in Action!

I want to share a powerful illustration of how both the layers we've discussed throughout this book and the Mindset Switch System come together to create transformation. Sharissa tells her story in her own words below, but I have made some notations so that you can see where all of the moving parts are. The story will take you through each step in the Mindset Switch System, where I have also pointed out where we can see each layer represented in Sharissa's transformation. (**W**ords, **T**houghts, **F**eelings, and **B**eliefs)

Because each person is unique, every personal transformation will look a little different. Your story might be a whole lot more about the words you use, or some deep-rooted beliefs that affect several areas of your life. Sharissa's story centers around both feelings and beliefs, and you can see how they were playing a role in the destruction of her power and then how she used those same layers to pull herself to a much better place.

### Sharissa's Transformation from Doormat to Decidedly Boss

### DISCOVER

I felt like I was failing. All. The. Time. **[F]** Working 50-60 hours a week. Trying to propel my new career as an entrepreneur. Working to facilitate new relationships and partnerships. But I didn't feel like I was making progress. I felt like a doormat. Like everyone around me was taking advantage of me. And I was allowing it. I was ashamed. **[F]**

But at the same time, I doubted my ability to succeed on my own. **[B]** I felt like even though these "partners" were taking advantage of me, that I owed them something. Loyalty? Time? As if my connection to them was what made me worthy.

I thought that maybe, if I stuck it out, it would pay off. **[B]** But that didn't happen. It just got worse. I felt like I was spinning in circles. Working harder and harder but getting nowhere. Clients came and went, but my income still wasn't consistent, and my business was stagnant.

## DREAM

I just wanted, for once, to feel like everything was moving in the right direction. I wanted to be respected, valued, taken seriously. **[W]** I wanted to be treated like a real person and a professional. I had big dreams written in my heart. My purpose was much, much bigger than my life trajectory at the time. **[F, B]** I knew I wanted to change lives on a large scale—to be the Tony Robbins of nutrition. I wanted everyone to know my name, my mission, and my work. And I wanted the time I spent with my clients and on my business to always feel fulfilling **[F]**. Somewhere deep down inside of me, I knew that was possible. **[B]**

But I also knew that the path I was on wasn't going to get me there.

## DECLUTTER

I knew I had to change my view of myself. Let go of the judgment and unreasonably high expectations. Stop judging myself as a failure. **[T]** I had to change how I was talking to and thinking about myself. **[W, T]** I remember asking myself, "Is this something you'd say to your daughter? Is this something you'd tolerate someone saying to your best friend?" If the answer was "NO!" then I knew I couldn't tolerate saying it to myself anymore, either. **[W]**

I started rephrasing the way I looked at failure by repositioning it as progress, which is actually a success! **[W]**

**DO**

Some days, that simply meant putting on clothes, getting out of the house and talking to people. It's the smallest accomplishments that add up to big wins!

The scariest thing I had to teach myself to do was lean into discomfort, to step out of my comfort zone consistently, and to experience the full range of emotions that come with that. **[F]** I had to remind myself that it's unrealistic to expect to be happy all the time. I had to learn that it's okay to be sad, depressed, angry, and disappointed because all those emotions are all a part of the growth process. **[B]** But that the important part is to keep showing up; to keep consistently working toward my purpose.

**DETACH**

The most empowering lesson I learned from going through the Mindset Switch System is how to detach and let go of my expectations. I remember writing down an affirmation that said, "I'm a writer, speaker, and teacher," because I wanted to do more speaking. **[W, B]** Within days, three offers to speak came in! I never worried about how those offers would come, I just set the intention, and they happened!

I am in such a good place now. I feel great, **[F]** and I'm no longer subjecting myself to the abuse of people around me. I am taking care of me first, listening to my intuition and my business is growing faster than ever! It's all about mindset. I truly believe that! **[B]**

Okay . . . Ahhhh, take a deeeeep breath. Seriously. Inhale slowly . . . And exhale.

You just took in a ton of information. You got vulnerable and looked within yourself to become a better version of you. But let's be honest, you were already fabulous and amazing in every way to begin with, you can just see it a little clearer now! Spend a moment to celebrate that. To celebrate you! And to celebrate your **why**— the reason you are choosing to do this work. It's true that I wrote this book and started this movement because of my mom. But you know who else is at the core of my "why?"

YOU!

You share something very special with every single person in the world: *unexplored possibilities.* I want to help you restore your belief that anything is possible! And as much as I would love to hang out in living rooms across the world sipping wine and chatting through all this, that's a little tricky, logistically speaking. But if I can inspire you to take action toward achieving your dreams, then it's just as impactful! Because I know you're not going to do this quietly. You are going to share what you've learned with someone else. Someone who, like you, has a beautiful light shining brightly inside of them, and an incredible about of potential. Someone who just needs a little nudge from a good friend (that's you!) to let their light shine.

Besides, anytime you set on an action-packed journey, especially the kind that involves life-altering, dream-building adventure, isn't it just more fun to bring a friend along?

And you know I'm all about taking action! So, you know I had to include a workbook.

This is it. Are you ready to level up your life? Let's do it!

Disempowering beliefs are what create the limits in your life, and empowering beliefs are what remove those limits.

When you shift your focus from what you cannot do and instead choose to focus on what you can do, your life will become limitless.

# Part 2:
## The Switch System Workbook

Now for the actionable part (which happens to be my favorite)! We've spent lots of time together diving into the layers of mindset and how they come together to create the beliefs and actions that result in life as we know it. But what if we want to change those results? What if we want a better reality? Simple. We choose new (better) words, thoughts, feelings, and beliefs, which then lead to empowered actions which lead to the desired results we're after.

Easy peasy. Right?

It is if you do the work. And because I'm an action girl, I've put together a few exercises that will familiarize you with the Mindset Switch System and get you on the fast track to achieving the life you want.

## How to make the most of this workbook:

**Take it one exercise at a time.** Bulldozing through these steps will dilute their impact. Instead, take it slow and allow yourself as much time as you need to fully process the questions and search within yourself for the honest, unbiased answers that surface.

**There are no right or wrong answers.** When it comes to reprogramming your mind for success, you might be tempted to hold back on some of these exercises. You might fear some of your answers (or someone seeing them). If that's the case, I invite you to use a separate sheet of paper or notebook and destroy it when you're finished, if that makes you feel more comfortable. The important thing here is that you don't hold back. This is an opportunity to bring your thoughts and emotions up to the surface and into your conscious awareness, which is necessary to effectively flip the switch on your mindset.

**Set aside time to tune in.** I recommend setting time aside where you know you'll be fully present. Most exercises can be done in less than 20 minutes, but if you'd like more time to work, by all means, allow yourself that luxury! Feel free to stretch these exercises out over a couple of days. Give yourself the time and space you need to effectively process this new information and notice how it shows up in the world around you. By connecting this new information to real-life scenarios, you'll be able to use it to your advantage!

**Set an intention for each exercise.** Before starting each exercise, take a moment to breathe and set an intention so that your focus is completely on the activity.

**Find an accountability partner.** I encourage you to find an accountability partner to work with, so you make sure to follow through but also to talk about any resistance that may come up in creating these changes.

**Have Fun!** Above all, have a little fun with this! Remember, joy is essential to maintaining a high vibe!

Whether you're doing these exercises as you go through each chapter, or you've chosen to work through them after you've completed reading the whole book, I want to welcome you to Step One of changing your life. Great job, rockstar!

# Step 1: Discover

## Do-Not-Want List

Limiting beliefs show up for us as results in our life. When we can identify the undesirable results we're currently getting, we have identified the starting point to change. This exercise will help you identify what really needs to change so you can start getting the results you want.

Pick an aspect of your life that you want to work on: Your home life, business, money, relationships, health, etc. Then, in regards to that aspect, ask yourself the following questions. Journal your responses in the space below.

- What words would best describe this aspect of my life?
- What isn't working for me in this aspect right now?
- What am I putting off? (You know that thing that's on your "Someday" list? Why isn't it on the "right now" list?)
- What do I say to myself about this aspect that isn't all that nice? What thoughts follow these statements? How does this make me feel?

Are you willing to take full responsibility for these things?

Are you ready to release the blame and accept that you have control?

Meditate on how your Do-Not-Want List makes you feel, and then release all of the toxic negativity those feelings bring, during your meditation. (download a guided meditation at www. TonyaRineer.com/ms-bonuses)

Proclaim that you are now ready to invite and allow positive words, thoughts, feelings, and ideas into your life with a new mantra or affirmation.

**My New Positive Affirmation is:**

## Mirror Work

This is a powerful exercise, inspired by one of my favorite spiritual teachers of all time, Louise Hay.

We are all guilty of saying things to ourselves that we would never say to a friend out loud. Why? Because we know how badly those words can hurt. Yet, we continue to be our own worst critic. We say (and think) way more negative things about ourselves than positive. This exercise is designed to interrupt the negative talk and tip the scales until our self-talk becomes more positive than negative.

Repeat step 4 of this process every day until you notice a breakthrough transformation. Trust me, after you get through the initial awkwardness, you'll love it! And it will change your life!

1. Let's start by identifying all the negative things say to yourself. In the left column below, write down everything that you might think or say to or about yourself when you're taking on the role of your Inner Critic. (This is the voice in your head that is incessantly reminding you of all the reasons you can't do it, or you're not good enough, and is forever pointing out your faults and flaws.)

Note: If brainstorming this list feels difficult, try stretching this exercise out over a couple of days. Anytime you notice yourself speaking (or thinking) negative self-talk, add the comment or phrase to this list. Once you've identified a few of your habitual phrases, then move on to step 2.

- What's wrong with you?
- What do you do wrong? What aren't you good at?
- What don't you like about yourself?
- What mean thing has someone said to you that you believed?
- What is it about your behavior that is less than desirable?
- What do you often wish you could change about yourself?

2. Now, let's step into the role of your Inner Cheerleader. (This is the voice of encouragement, support, and compassion. The one that reminds you of how amazing you are and loves to point out your strengths and superpowers) If your Inner Cheerleader were to argue with your Inner Critic and try to prove her wrong, what would you say? In the right column, write three nice things for every negative thing you wrote down in the Inner Critic column.

3.  Now, see all those things you wrote in that first column? Cross it out! Or, if you did this exercise on a separate sheet of paper, rip it off and burn it! Not a single thing on that list is true! They're lies, and they're not worth hanging on to.

4.  Ok, now for my favorite part! Go to the mirror. Look yourself in the eye and say those nice things to yourself. Just like you're saying them to a friend. Go ahead, do it! I know it feels awkward. So what? Do it anyway! Trust me; you'll thank me later.

| My Inner Critic Says... | My Inner Chearleader Says... |
| --- | --- |
| | |

# Step 2: Dream

Now that you've identified what's not working for you and what you no longer want (or are willing to tolerate) let's get hyper-focused on what it is you do want.

You may want to begin this exercise by visualizing, in vivid detail, what your dream life looks like six months, one year or three years from now. (You can access a guided visualization for this at www.tonyarineer.com/ms-bonuses)

Then, put the details of that dream life on paper. I love desire mapping and dream boards for this! Both, when finished, act as visual reminders of what it is that you truly desire (and deserve) and help to keep you focused on what's possible for you.

## Dream Map

I love, love, love dream mapping! It works just like mind-mapping, where you brainstorm ideas onto paper.

How do create your desire map:

1.   Get a piece of paper and a pencil. Draw a circle in the center of your paper.

2.   Choose one area of your life you'd like to concentrate on for this exercise (business, money, relationships, personal development, health, spirituality, etc.). Write it in the center of the circle. In the example shown, I chose Business.

3.   Next, start brainstorming all of the goals or desires you have for that aspect of your life. Write them down around your center

circle. (My desires are: Make $100k a year, write a book, become a speaker, start a podcast). Next, circle each of those desires and then draw a line that connects the desire to the center circle.

4. Now, next to each desire, ask yourself: Why, do I want this? How will this make me feel? And continue to extend your map outward until you've identified the emotional why behind each desire.

I love desire mapping because it connects you to the real desire, which is not the thing or the accomplishment itself, but the underlying feeling you're craving. This is a very eye-opening exercise and helps to fast-track the realization of your dreams and desire. Simply by connecting the desired emotion it holds. Plus, it's fun!

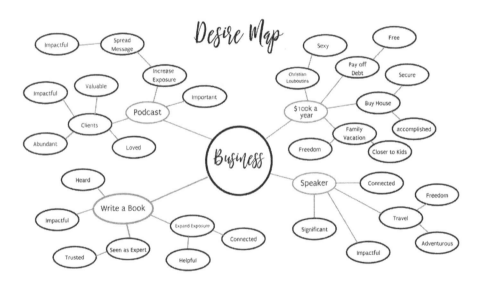

## Vision Board

A vision board is a visual representation of your dreams, desires, and intentions.

To create one for yourself, you'll need a large poster board, a variety of old magazines (Real Simple, HGTV, Yoga Journal, Parenting Magazine, Travel, Dwell, etc.), scissors and glue.

Begin looking through the magazines and cutting out anything that represents your dream life. You might find images that represent your dream home, dream car, and vacations you dream of taking. You might choose visual representations of your children attending their favorite college or your husband golfing more (because that's what he loves to do). Your images might include a magazine cover (to represent a goal of being featured in a magazine), or the name of your favorite charity (because you'd like to be more involved with it). Whatever you dream of, find a visual representation of it. The key here is not necessarily to find something that looks exactly like the things you desire, but that when you look at the picture, it makes you feel something.

Once you've got all your images selected, glue them to your poster board. Let that baby dry and hang it where you'll be able to see it every day.

Need ideas? Pinterest has a ton of inspirational dream and vision boards you can check out. Or check out my Pinterest board for a collection of inspiration at https://www.pinterest.com/tonyarineer/vision-board-ideas/

**Extra Credit:** My favorite activity is to combine the two exercises above. Start by visualizing your dream life, then do the Desire Map exercise to get all of your desires and desired emotions onto paper. Then, put together a pretty dream board of visuals and images that is representative of both the things you want and the feelings you desire. Talk about powerful!

# Step 3: Declutter

Before we can declutter, you have to ask yourself: What is your level of expectation, on a scale of 1-10, that everything you dream of is possible for you?

1-------2-------3-------4-------5-------6-------7-------8-------9-------10

If your answer is any less than an 8, why? Seriously, ask yourself why. Be honest with yourself. The answers might surprise you (and they might even scare you a little), but they will be very, very enlightening!

## PINPOINT, PURGE AND PROVE

1. WHY: List all the reasons why your **dream** life isn't possible for you right now.

Before we move on, physically cross out all the reasons that suggest your dream isn't possible. Those are lies! You are entitled to every one of the things you wrote down! And doing this work is going to help you make those dreams your reality. You with me? Ok, good. Moving on . . .

2. WHAT: Examine the list you just created and begin assessing what's really going on beneath the surface by asking these questions:

- What excuses do you need to let go of?
- What toxic people do you need to distance yourself from?
- What words do you need to change?
- What in your environment needs to go?
- In what way have you set unrealistic and unfair expectations of . . .
    - Yourself
    - Success
- What is a more realistic and graceful expectation?

The Mindset Switch

3. HOW: How can you prove to yourself (and your brain) that it really is possible?

```
┌─────────────────────────────────────────────┐
│                                             │
│                                             │
│                                             │
│                                             │
│                                             │
│                                             │
│                                             │
│                                             │
│                                             │
└─────────────────────────────────────────────┘
```

Identify and record any proof that exists that shows you that what you desire is possible. Your brain looooves patterns and proof. It likes a story—a beginning, middle, and end. You're in the middle of your story now (it's the change part!). The end is the desired result, and the inevitable successful outcome you'll achieve (yay!). But if your brain is having trouble believing in a happy ending, try giving it some tried and true proof to buy into.

What have you already accomplished or done in your life that is evidence that this desire is possible and attainable for you?

If you don't have proof in your own life, use someone else's proof. Do a little research. How many stories can you find of other people who started in a similar situation as yours? What you find will be inspiring at worst and transformational at best. Either way, it's a win-win exercise!

*Hint: If you get stuck, ask for help inside our Facebook group at www.TonyaRineer.com/facebook. We all love a homework challenge in that group!*

# Step 4: Do

The thing about taking action toward success is that one small step at a time is all you need to take. And that's all you need to focus on. Big, overarching visions are cool and all, and they can help you map out your final destination, but visions don't create results. Action creates results.

There are two ways to motivate someone to take action: Avoid pain or seek pleasure. The following exercises will help you tap into feelings of pleasure through experiencing quick, but powerful wins.

## Baby Steps to Success

I'm a big visionary. So if you struggle with chunking things down into bite-sized pieces, I totally get it. (I do too!) I'm going to make it super easy for you. We'll take it slow and go one step at a time.

1. What are all the big steps that need to happen for you to get to your desire?

2. Number those steps according to what you feel should happen first, second, third, etc. Don't worry about getting this right. You can change this sequence as often as you need to. For this exercise, it's not important to have all the answers, or the sequencing, right.

3. For the action step that you marked as number one, what smaller action steps need to happen in order to accomplish that first big step (or milestone)? How will accomplishing those smaller, baby steps make you feel?

4. If these baby steps still feel out of your element and scary, break them down even further. Keep doing this until they feel doable and exciting.

5. Commit to taking one action step, within the next 24 hours, that will accomplish the following:

- Move you closer to your goal

- Help you tap into your core desired feelings (the ones you identified in the Dream phase)

6. How will you know if you were successful? What will you feel once you've taken this baby action step? What will success look and feel like? What will it mean for you?

By the way, this should feel slightly uncomfortable. Remember, it should feel like a stretch but not a strain.

## Emotional Success Journaling

This one is so easy it's mind-blowing. But, it's crazy effective. Here's how it works:

Allow yourself 10 minutes every day to journal your response to the following questions:

Today was awesome because . . .

I learned . . .

I am proud of myself because . . .

I am grateful for . . .

Tomorrow, I'm looking forward to . . .

The Mindset Switch

The exercises above will put you back in the driver's seat of your life. They help give you back the control and the power to feel good on demand. That's because doing these exercises will connect you to feelings of joy, love, gratitude, and abundance—all of which will align you with the highest possible vibration there is. After doing these exercises, you will feel lighter, empowered, inspired and grounded. Some people report feeling closer to God (or Source Energy, or the Universe, or whatever high power you connect to) after working through these activities.

Here's the thing, though, those feelings wear off. If you want to stay aligned with your high vibe, you have to engage in exercises like these on a regular basis. I recommend 5-10 minutes every morning and 10-30 minutes every night (at a minimum). And anytime you feel your vibration dip down below Awesome, give yourself a few minutes to take a break, engage in a few minutes of feel-good, vibe-raising activity to reset yourself and then go back to your regular day. Do this for thirty days, and you will feel like a new person. Guaranteed!

# Step 5: Detach

Are you willing to let go of control over what needs to happen and how? Your only "job" is to decide what doesn't work, what you want instead, declutter what's not serving you, and take small micro-sized baby steps (one at a time) toward your desired feelings. This final step requires no effort on your part. Instead, you just get to surrender to the Universe and allow the awesomeness to happen. But first, you need to detach!

On a scale of 1-10, how detached are you from the outcome? (The closer to 10 you can get, the better!)


1-------2-------3-------4-------5-------6-------7-------8-------9-------10


Surrendering to the Universe and opening yourself up to allowing abundance into your life has nothing to do with hustle or effort, and everything to do with maintaining your feel-good vibe by doing things that feel good to you.

Wait? What!?!? I know. It's almost too simple to be real. Especially if you're of the mindset that anything worthwhile takes hard work. This doesn't. The hard work is already done.

When you tune into what's not working, allow yourself the space to dream of new possibilities, make the changes necessary to better yourself, and take action, you're 90% to the goal of manifesting your dream life! This last part—the allowing—is the simple part. You just get to feel good and let it happen.

## Good Vibrations

1. Tuning into good vibrations requires you to engage in activities and do things that make you feel good. What are those things? This exercise is designed to help you recognize (and engage in) the things that raise your vibe and help you feel amazing. Let's identify what those things are.

Things and activities that make me feel **joy** are . . .

Things and activities that make me feel **empowered** are . . .

Things and activities that make me feel **love** are . . .

Things and activities that make me feel **appreciation** are . . .

2. Commit to do something from one of the lists above each week. (Bonus points for making an appointment with yourself and scheduling it in the calendar!)

## Down the Rabbit Hole

I'd love to tell you that everything you desire will happen exactly how and when you want it to. But that's just not the case. The Universe works in mysterious ways. And when you follow the Mindset Switch System, your desires will indeed manifest, but sometimes, not in the way you imagined.

Instead of worrying and stressing over the "how" and "when," allow yourself to be open to possibilities and pleasant surprises and let the Universe do its thing.

To help you get more comfortable with this process, ask yourself the following questions:

What do I fear the most about this not working "how" and "when" I want?

What will it say about me if this doesn't work out?

What will happen if this doesn't work out? What is the worst-case scenario?

How will I handle it if that happens?

How can I plan and prepare myself for the worst outcome, just in case?

How will I bounce back and keep going? (How have I done this in the past?)

How will I be better as a result of overcoming the worst-case outcome?

Do I believe that this will really happen?

What is likely to happen instead?

What amazing things will remain unchanged in my life, either way?

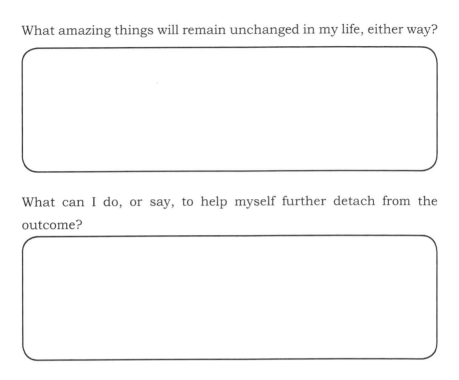

What can I do, or say, to help myself further detach from the outcome?

Wow! Take a minute and celebrate all the work you just finished! You are such a rockstar! So many people don't finish the books they pick up. They don't take the time to stop and reflect. But you did all that, and you completed the workbook! That says something extraordinary about you. It says that you're not going to wish your dream life into reality, you're going to take control and make it happen!

In the name of celebrating, this seems like the perfect time to show yourself a little love. What's your new favorite high-vibe activity? Do that right now! I love a good living room dance party, so feel free to use that one. Because that's most likely what I'm doing, too! (You didn't think I was going to let you celebrate all by yourself, did you?)

# A FINAL INVITATION

After you get through with a few high-vibe moments to celebrate yourself, I'd love for you to join my private Facebook community at **www.tonyarineer.com/facebook** where every week we come up with creative ways to #fliptheswitch, and everyday's a party! It's also where we want to hear all about your a-ha moments, transformative realizations, and favorite parts of this book. We are here to support you in continuing on this journey! Because as you know, this is only the beginning of a whole new life. It only gets better from here!

# Part 3
## Mastermind Questions

Did you know that the best way to retain what you learn is by reteaching it? This book is a powerful tool for teaching you how to flip the switch on your mindset. And, according to research on learning retention, you'll likely retain 10% of what you read. Because I really do want you to walk away with transformative results, I've provided Mastermind Questions for you below, so that you can take what you've learned in the book one step further. Use this book as an outline for your Mastermind Group or Book Club. Simply by talking through these questions, you're likely to retain 50% of what you learned here.

If you want the most bang for your buck, though, I suggest you complete the workbook! And once you've done that, and you begin to experience the profound results of a positive mindset—you know, manifesting your desires, feeling pretty awesome about yourself, taking inspired action and enjoying the process of expansion—I invite you to take it one step further, still, and teach what you're learning with others.

Use these Mastermind questions to teach others how to create their own Mindset Switch and you will retain a whopping 90% of what you learned, which is pretty awesome. But moreover, you'll be making an impact on the world by helping others improve their mindset, realize what's really possible for them, and take back the power to create the life they've always wanted.

As much as I'd love to reach and help everyone, I just can't do it alone. But with your help, we can change the world, together!

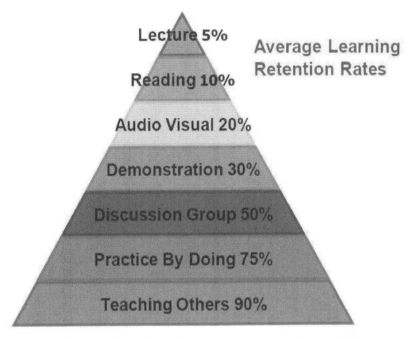

Source: National Training Laboratories, Bethel, Maine

**Chapter 1:**

1. When were you first introduced to the concept of mindset management? Was this a concept you were familiar with growing up?

2. Explain the connection, as you see it, between self-worth and success.

3. Describe a time when you defeated the odds or made a conscious choice to succeed in the face of a challenge.

## Chapter 2:

1. Have you explored the idea of limited vs. growth mindsets before? In what context(s) have you heard about it? How does limited or growth mindset (or both) show up in your life?

2. Share your "why." What is your bigger purpose to understanding mindset and what are you hoping to gain in doing so?

## Chapter 3:

1. Discuss your previous knowledge of and experience with the Laws of Attraction and Vibration. Discuss any preconceived notions you have or used to have about these concepts.

2. Think about your own "wooden chair" example. When in your life have you become aware of a "blind spot" because of your brain's focus on a certain outcome?

3. What would you like to attract more of into your life?

## Chapter 4:

1. What areas of your life are stagnant? What areas of your life are thriving? How do you think about those areas differently?

2. Are there people, places or activities in your life that are triggering you to think, feel and act in ways that are detrimental to your success? Briefly discuss them with the group.

3. What about people, places or activities that light you up and empower you? Discuss them as well.

## Chapter 5:

1. Discuss your response to the quote: "You get to shift from life

happens to me, to life happens because of me." How does that feel for both the exciting parts AND the challenging parts of life?

2. Name something that has been on your "someday" list that you're committed to making a current priority. How will you hold yourself accountable for making it happen?

3. Share your Do-Not-Want List with the group. What did you learn about yourself when creating this list?

4. Discuss your immediate response to the concept of "layers" introduced in this chapter. How do these layers (words, thoughts, feelings, and beliefs) offer a new perspective on how you live your life?

**Chapter 6:**

1. What words do you need to remove from your vocabulary? Ask your group to keep you accountable.

2. Get real about how you talk to yourself. Do you set the intention to build yourself up or do you get caught in the web of negative self-talk?

3. Share some of your new "Braffirmations" with your group.

**Chapter 7:**

1. Consider the quote: "The way we think about ourselves ultimately determines our self-worth. And our self-worth determines how resistant or open to possibilities we are. And that resistance or openness determines our reality." Have you considered the power of your self-worth in this way before? On a scale of 1-10, how much do you believe this to be true?

2. We tend to think of building ourselves up as egotistical, self-

centered, and maybe even narcissistic. Change that idea and fill in the blank with something different. "Building myself up with daily affirming thoughts is _____." (examples: empowering, essential, powerful, etc.)

3. Create your own braffirmation. Discuss the way this mantra summons up memories that support your desires.

## Chapter 8:

1. Discuss the Law of Vibration and how it connects with feelings. How do you notice a mind/body shift from negative feelings (victimized, unworthy, shame, guilt) to positive ones (gratitude, generosity, love, joy)?

2. Discuss the concept that an emotion only lasts for 90 seconds. How does that change your perspective on how feelings affect you?

3. Share an area where you can shift from a negative feeling to a positive one today. (Use the Emotional Guidance Scale as a reference.)

## Chapter 9:

1. What excuse do you find yourself using the most? What is the real reason behind why you're making this excuse?

2. Identify and discuss an activity that always seems to lighten your mood and move you higher up on the emotional scale.

## Chapter 10:

1. Identify a couple of your limiting beliefs and work on discovering their origin.

(Were you taught something in childhood that created a limiting belief? A traumatic event? Relentless repetition?)

2. Share some items from your Dream Life brain dump. Answer the question: What's stopping you from having that right now? Notice any blocks that come up and discuss with the group.

## Chapter 11:

1. Discover – Discuss a couple of areas of your life that aren't working the way you want them to.

2. Dream – Share your big ideas on how you would love your life to look.

3. Declutter – What do you need to let go of or get rid of to move toward your dreams? Help each other stay accountable.

4. Do (something!) – What is an action step you will commit to taking today? Be specific and check back in with each other to insure follow through.

5. Detach – Share how detached you are from the outcome you want on a scale from 1-10. What activities will you engage in to align yourself with high-vibe energy? Help each other get to a 10 through emotional vibration work.

# Thank You

Once upon a time, a little girl had a big dream to write a book that would change the lives of many. What this little girl learned while pursuing that dream is that it really does take a village! This book is in your hands right now for one reason only: Because you helped make it possible!

Tara Bosler, my writing partner, without you my words would still be jumbles of chaos scattered around in my head and on the pages of a dozen different notebooks.

Alexa Bigwarfe, Liz Thompson and Michelle Fairbanks, my incredible book team, thank you for pushing me beyond my limits, raising the bar and working tirelessly to make this dream happen.

This could have never happened without my work family— The hustlers who show up and work nonstop behind the scenes to keep everything running smoothly, I honestly don't know what I'd do without you. Danielle Roberts, Raewyn Sangari and Daniel Rameros, I appreciate all you do.

And to my coaches, John Schamante and Dana Malstaff who believed in my ability to share this message with the world and my mentors, Hal Elrod and Jon Berghoff for showing me what is possible when you choose a to surround yourself with a "family" of like-minded, positive thinkers. Thank you for helping me see, and believe in, endless possibilities!

Before every final draft is not-so-pretty rough draft. Stacy Firth, Alecia St. Germain, Mallory Schlabach, Judy Mannino, Tiffany

Cavegn, Mike Rineer, Danelle DeCarlo, Sharissa Bradley and Rob Arnold, every one of your comments and suggestions was received with love and implemented with gratitude. This book wouldn't be what it is without your unconditional support and impressive genius!

I'd love to say that I kicked back and chillaxed on a beach somewhere while leisurely bringing these words to life. But, I live in the real world and there were more than a few days where I leaned heavily on the support of my inner circle to be my sounding board, to feed me (when I forgot to eat), to make me laugh when I needed a break and cheer me on when I needed a pep rally. My husband Tom, my incredible sons, Kyle, Matthew, and Tommy, my sister, Danelle, my aunt Judy Mannino and my besties, Steve Sinishtaj and Maria Vera, thank you for your unconditional love, support and encouragement. I love you.

To my clients, thank you for giving me the greatest gift of all—your trust. I feel truly honored to have shared in your journey and watching you succeed is one of my greatest pleasures. Your ambition, strength and accomplishments continue to inspire me. I have deep gratitude and love for each and every one of you!

One of the things I look forward to most everyday is checking in with the Party Peeps inside of the Profit Party Facebook community. The vibe and energy that exists there is mind-blowing and contagious. It's one of my favorite places to be. The way you rally around and support one another is truly magical. You are the most incredible group of women I know and I am so grateful for each and every one of you. I love you all to pieces! XO

And to YOU. . . for reading this book. For taking the time to invest in yourself and make a commitment to take control of the life you were always meant to live—the life that's full of endless possibilities, unimaginable success and limitless abundance.

# About the Author

Tonya Rineer is a Speaker, Trainer, Money Mindset and Business Coach who helps women entrepreneurs connect the dots between self-worth and success. Her action-oriented and high-energy style is a holistic blend of intuitive mindset work and practical strategy that empowers women to live their truth, do what feels good and live a life of financial abundance.

Learn more about Tonya at http://tonyarineer.com and join her active Facebook group for more mindset help and support at http://tonyarineer.com/facebook.

Printed in Great Britain
by Amazon

38466061R00129